DISCARD

The Hero
in French Romantic Literature

The Hero
in French Romantic Literature

by
George Ross Ridge

University of Georgia Press

To

JAMES M. SMITH
Emory University

MAXWELL A. SMITH
University of Chattanooga

and

HOWARD SUTTON
Vanderbilt University

CONTENTS

Preface   ix

   THE ROOTS OF ROMANTICISM   1

I THE SEEKER   15

II THE MAN OF FATE   32

III HYPERSENSIBILITY AND THE PATHOLOGICAL HERO   53

IV THE POET-PROPHET   75

V THE REBEL AND THE DANDY   96

VI THE ANTI-HERO   115

   CONCLUSION   129

Notes   138

Index   143

PREFACE

IS ANOTHER study of French romanticism justified?

I asked myself this same question, years ago, when I first became interested in the romantic hero. Surely the bibliographies, after a hundred years of research and polemics, must fairly bulge with articles, books, manifestoes, and *explications de texte*. Yet as I began to move more deeply into the subject, I realized with astonishment that, despite all previous research, the romantic hero himself—the very key to understanding the spirit of romanticism—had been strangely neglected. Only Mario Praz, in his *Romantic Agony,* and a mere handful of other writers in widely scattered pages seem to have studied the romantic hero at all; and their observations have been mostly descriptive, not analytic. There was a great need, it seemed to me, first for close analysis, then for synthesis. The dark soul of the romantic hero had remained largely unprobed, and to that extent he was, indeed, still a man of mystery.

Hence *The Hero in French Romantic Literature* is intended to fill a historical gap in the scholarship of romanticism. It is an attempt to define the hero and to trace his principal lines of descent throughout the romantic movement proper. In my study I was forced to draw a fairly surprising conclusion: The romantic hero is essentially the same man as he moves through romantic poems, plays, stories, and novels, in spite of the most seeming variations. Basically the romantic hero is the same man, not a series of protagonists with different aspirations and modes of behavior. The variations of the hero are, in fact, subsumed by an idea of the archetypal hero—the self-conscious hero, as I chose to name him.

By the *self-conscious hero* I refer to the essence of the romantic protagonist, after his many various trappings have been stripped away. He is what remains beneath a multitude of poses and superficial traits. He is at once a reflection of the romantic writer and a projection of what the romantics considered the *ideal man,* for any hero must be, by definition, a concept of the ideal man. By studying the romantic hero in this light we can visualize, to a rather fine point, just what sort of configuration the romantic ideal man assumed.

Thus a study of the romantic hero can tell us much about the spirit of the age. He can lead us straight to the writer's own psyche, as both an artistic reflection and projection. He can reveal the values which motivate the hero and characterize the romantic worldview. For he will surely reflect the writer's beliefs and ideas, as he is caught up in the social cataclysm and philosophical reorientation of romanticism. Surely, then, the romantic hero is our best touchstone to understanding romantic literature.

My debts have been many in the preparation of this book.

I am primarily indebted to Dr. James M. Smith (Emory University) for suggesting the subject and offering me the wealth of his vast reading and knowledge. His criticism has been invaluable. I owe a debt of affection as well as gratitude to Dr. Maxwell A. Smith (University of Chattanooga) and Dr. Howard Sutton (Vanderbilt University) for their continued interest in all my work throughout the years. Their suggestions have always been exact and just.

I want to express my gratitude to Dr. Ward Pafford and

Dr. Walter A. Strauss, both of Emory University, for reading
and criticizing the manuscript during the various stages of
its preparation. I am also grateful to Dr. R. H. Anacker
(University of Chattanooga), Dr. Elizabeth Barineau (University of Chicago), Dr. William Beardslee (Emory University), Dr. Howard E. Hugo (Brooklyn College), and Mrs.
Edith Karush (Emory University) for reading earlier drafts
of the manuscript and offering their valuable comments.

I want to thank Mr. Ralph Stephens, director of the University of Georgia Press, for his continued interest and scholarly
advice. Thanks are also due Dr. Julian Harris (University
of Wisconsin), editor of *The French Review,* for permission
to include some material which appeared in my article "The
Anti-Hero in Musset's Drama," *The French Review* (April
1959).

And to my wife, Davy, I owe a special debt, for without
her presence, encouragement, and suggestions this work
would never have been completed.

GEORGE ROSS RIDGE

23 March 1959
Atlanta, Georgia

THE ROOTS OF ROMANTICISM

ROMANTICISM is the point of departure in modern literature. Most critics accept this statement although few agree on a definition for romanticism and although they assess the romantic movement with diverse and vehement partisanship. Confusion about the essence of romanticism is moreover present among the romantic writers themselves. Consider for example the following definitions:[1]

Sénancour: Le romantisme est une sensibilité forte, simple, primitive, s'exprimant en un style, libre, inégal, irrégulier.

Stendhal: Le romantisme est une littérature qui donne le plus de plaisir possible aux modernes; le classicisme, celle qui donnait le plus grand plaisir possible à leurs arrière-grands-pères.

Desprès: Le romantisme est le transport du spiritualisme dans la littérature.

Vitet: C'est le protestantisme dans les lettres et dans les arts.

Deschamps: C'est la poésie, le classicisme étant la prose.—Ou encore: le romantisme, c'est le nouveau.

Soumet: C'est la littérature des émotions.

Guiraud: C'est le vrai relatif; c'est le moi, c'est le coeur, ennemis de l'ordre, de la correction et du goût.

1

Hugo: C'est la vérité dans la forme, le mélange des genres, la
  liberté dans l'art, le libéralisme en littérature.
Nodier: C'est le goût du merveilleux et du fantastique.
Musset: C'est l'abus des adjectifs.

It is evident that several definitions are serious while others
are ironic; Musset's intent is obviously not that of Sénancour.
Such definitions are further disconcerting since they indicate
more about the writer than about the movement itself and
since many of the writers elsewhere define romanticism in a
different way.

Their confusion is understandable. While historical per-
spective is necessary for a clear appraisal of a movement, the
romantics are personally involved in the spirit of their age.
Perhaps the confusion continues largely because post-romantic literature, like realism, symbolism, and naturalism, tends
to develop certain romantic themes.[2] But however the movement is defined, both romantic writers and critics realize
that the literature of the period is unique, and they self-
consciously attempt to explain its goals and methods.

A definition, however tentative, is necessary to establish
the nomenclature of any meaningful study. Literary boundary lines, while of very limited value for romanticism,[3] are
still indispensable. An epistemological difficulty is apparent;
an enumeration of salient characteristics does not in itself
afford an understanding of a phenomenon. Barzun illustrates
this point by arguing that[4]

. . . romanticism is not a return to the Middle Ages, a love of
the exotic, a revolt from Reason, a vindication of the individual,
a liberation of the unconscious, a reaction against scientific
method, a revival of pantheism, idealism, and catholicism, a
rejection of artistic conventions, a preference for emotion, a
movement back to nature, or a glorification of force.

For these traits are not uniformly present in the romantic
writers.

Romanticism is a worldview in which the individual romantic works are rooted, but it is uncertain whether the
romantic worldview results from cataclysm or evolution.

Robertson believes that romanticism "may be seen disso-
ciating itself from the classic canon by a slow and difficult
process," that the romantic doctrine is "no less a daughter of
the Renaissance than the faith of Boileau himself."[5] Girard
argues that "le véritable Romantisme—le Romantisme pure-
ment littéraire—s'introduit modestement dans la littérature."[6]
Deschamps states in a romantic manifesto: "Il n'y a réelle-
ment pas de romantisme, mais bien une littérature du dix-
neuvième siècle."[7] And some attempt to trace the roots of
romanticism to Plato and Christ. But whether these propositions are valid or not, it is clear that romanticism receives
its immediate impetus and emerges as a definable movement
with the new science, the industrial revolution, and a shift
in philosophical thought. Romantic literature differs from
classical literature, then, primarily because it is conceived
and nurtured in a different kind of society. From this standpoint romanticism is more cataclysmic than evolutionary.

Pascal, whom Barzun considers the father of modern romanticism,[8] first enunciates the philosophical basis of the
movement. By distinguishing between the *esprit de finesse*
and the *esprit de géométrie,* he contrasts the intuitive and the
analytical minds. He states that each characterizes a different
kind of knowledge. The *esprit de géométrie* knows analyti-
cally through discursive reason while the *esprit de finesse*
supersedes reason by adding intuition to the concept of human understanding. By arguing that the *esprit de géométrie*
does not utilize intuition, Pascal attacks a weakness in the
geometrical mind and particularly in Aristotelian logic.

Consider for instance the science of mathematics, which is
at once a mode of thinking and refusing to think. If one postulates certain assumptions, he may thereby deduce an entire
mathematical system. But since the system rests ultimately
upon an elaborate, deductive expansion of the original pre-
suppositions, he never achieves any basic new insights. This
is a weakness of the deductive method, which exemplifies
like mathematics the classic *esprit de géométrie.* Romantic
literature makes this criticism implicitly. The Kantian esthetic is moreover rooted in the romantic distinction between

knowing and *knowing about*,[9] and the mathematical method is for the moment discarded and later reinterpreted. For mathematics, the preferred science of the classic mind, works essentially with the equation and says in essence that $A=B+C$. However, the romantic writers are dissatisfied with the equation, since they believe, so to speak, that the whole may be greater than the sum of its parts.

In the romantic era science moves from the mathematical to a biological frame of reference. In a process of dissolution since the seventeenth century, classical mechanics now disintegrates.[10] Romanticism emphasizes the organism in its structure and function. It does not expect to discover absolute truth through dissection and analysis since it believes that life-force is an unknown factor in the organism. The romantic sense of mystery results from the belief that the essence of the organism is beyond human understanding. When deduction is fruitless, intuition alone can provide insight, and mysticism accompanies the romantic sense of mystery. In contrast with the seventeenth century romanticism accepts poetic as well as scientific truth.

In the classic and romantic periods the basic goal of the thinker is to determine man's place in the universe. But the fundamental assumptions and epistemological positions are different. The classic assumes that he can know the universe since his mind is an adequate organ of investigation. The romantic assumes that he can know the universe only imperfectly since his mind is an imperfect organ of perception. He questions his faculties of cognition; subjectivity is the result. Man does not know the universe; he knows only his own sense-impressions. Through subjectivity science becomes increasingly self-conscious, or, rephrased, science is subjective because it is self-conscious. For self-consciousness and subjectivity interact upon each other, and in both instances the mind investigates itself from an epistemological concern. Subjectivity has marked effects upon romantic thinking. A romantic like Coleridge postulates the unconscious mind, and nineteenth-century science early begins to foreshadow the Heisenberg uncertainty principle. Moreover, a touchstone to subjectivity is intuition, which the romantics feel is a valid if indefinable mode of understanding.

Romantic self-consciousness results from the social cataclysm[11] as well as from the new philosophical orientation. First, the French Revolution disrupts the continuity between generations by closing the salons and colleges. Since it snaps the traditional link between the old and the new, the young romantics are able to examine themselves more searchingly than would be possible in a society where the bonds are yet intact. Second, the Napoleonic period is a time of great enthusiasm and despair. As the reflection of a supreme egotist *lamb-* it marks an entire generation of egotistic men. Third, the industrial revolution, which is under way, helps disrupt the hierarchical society by making money the ultimate arbiter of social position. Men who are reared in one class become suddenly aware that their position in society has changed. They all react to this era of friction and change as they strive to find a niche in the new society. Many romantics participate in the political scene while others tend to withdraw. A definite correlation exists between the social cataclysm and the romantic movement as men search their souls in the midst of flux and fortune.[12]

Both romantic philosophy and the social cataclysm converge in individualism, which results from and also contributes to self-consciousness. The discovery of the unique self is a goal of romantic introspection, and Maigron observes that two factors dominate the romantic individualist—"l'hypertrophie de l'imagination et . . . la sensibilité."[13] With the philosophical and social background in mind Clement posits that "romanticism is imagination and feeling in rebellion against reason and will."[14] Such a historical cadre results in romantic sensibility, an aspect of individualism and a product of self-consciousness.

But semantic difficulties are apparent in the romantic notion of self-consciousness. *Imagination,* for example, is identified with fancy, with the artistic faculty, and with intuitive understanding. *Sensibility* is used literally to refer to patterns of emotional response, or it replaces *hypersensibility* as a word. Moreover, reason is classic rationalism or romantic understanding, for the romantics are not necessarily anti-rationalists:[16]

. . . Romanticism is not, as the world keeps parroting, a revolt from Reason, an emotional fling, an escape from the real. It is a voyage of discovery with the whole man as master. His reason, inseparably linked to his will, guides his desires and conserves the fruits of his action.

At least in theory the romantic writer interprets rather than refutes the function of reason. *Sensibility*, however, is the keyword since it is involved in the concept of self-consciousness; indeed sensibility and self-consciousness are inextricably linked. The hero has a romantic sensibility which the herdman does not possess, and he is self-conscious because he is aware of this fundamental difference between himself and the herdman. Romantic self-consciousness is not merely self-awareness or even the acute soul-searching which characterizes the age; self-consciousness rather includes the romantic sensibility in the hero's self-awareness. The romantic hero is self-consciously unique; he knows that he is different from and does not belong to the herd, to society. He is, in truth, outside society. It is in this respect that the romantic hero is the self-conscious hero, who differs from earlier hero-types.

These semantic considerations make romanticism and the romantic hero difficult to define. But it is nonetheless clear that romanticism is historically a different orientation in worldview and that the new philosophical direction is reflected in romantic literature by the different meanings ascribed to keywords like *reason, will, imagination, creativity, genius,* and *nature.* It is also clear that just as the philosophical and social roots of romanticism are correlated with the growth in self-consciousness, so the psychological traits of the romantic hero are an expression of self-consciousness. The philosophical and social roots are concretely expressed in the hero. And while the romantic movement may be defined as the acute quickening of self-consciousness of man in society, romantic literature is especially concerned with the extraordinary man—the romantic hero.

II

THREE ROMANTIC HEROES

There are two advantages in sketching prototypes of the romantic hero at this point. First, the character depictions emphasize the heroes' different traits and at the same time illustrate their basic similarity of type. Second, it is possible to discover from them a common denominator which serves as a key in this study of the hero. There is a profusion of examples. But Chateaubriand's René, Hugo's Hernani, and Balzac's Louis Lambert, romantic heroes from the works of the same name, have been selected since each illustrates certain traits of the hero-type. The following sketches are of course descriptive rather than analytic.

It is significant that the *mal de René* is synonymous with the *mal du siècle,* for no other hero epitomizes the romantic type so well as René. As the personification of the "vague des passions" in *Le Génie du christianisme,* René plays a dual role. He is both seeker and wanderer. But as a result of his "vague des passions" he is a searcher without a goal, unable to explain himself or diagnose his malady. As a seeker he does not know what he is looking for, and as a wanderer he does not know where he is going. His imagination is to blame since it evokes greater realities than he can find in actual life. The real world is not equal to the appetite of his romantic imagination and sensibility.

René recounts the story of his life to Chactas, a wise Indian chief in Louisiana. He is prompted to break his self-imposed silence by a letter from a French Mother Superior who expresses her condolences that his sister, Amélie, has died of a plague she contracted while caring for the sick. René must speak.

Even as a child he is inscrutable. He leaves his young companions to go aside and contemplate nature; his typical mood is *rêverie.* He burns from his imagination and finds peace only with his older sister, Amélie, but even she cannot offer a meaning for life.

His imagination prompts him to turn to Greece and Rome.

The ravages of time make life seem futile, for he extracts no meaning from their ruins and monuments. He turns to his contemporaries, but he finds nothing beautiful in the modern world after discovering nothing certain in the ancient world. He is preyed upon by his vague longings and sensations. He has no home.

Suddenly Amélie abandons him to an awful solitude. In a letter she recommends marriage for him and explains that she herself is retiring to a convent to become a nun. René follows her, pained and confused, but she refuses to see him. In the absence of their father, however, he is to fill the paternal role in her dedication. He resigns himself with some bitterness and much confusion. During the service René overhears Amélie pray in an undertone that God protect him from her criminal passion. She is in love with her own brother. He is shocked by this confession. Finally understanding why she left him, he embraces Amélie. She collapses in the confusion and is carried away, while he remains before the altar shouting and half-insane.

He decides to leave Europe and takes a ship for the New World, where he hopes to find happiness and contentment with the noble savages. He typifies the civilized man; he is characterized by spleen and ennui; and he turns to primitive man in his effort to find meaning in life. His rich imagination disenchants him; nothing lives up to his expectation. Consequently, his sensibility turns in upon itself, and he feels bitterness, frustration, defeat.

Chateaubriand condemns the man with whom he so evidently sympathizes.

Victor Hugo's Hernani is a Spanish nobleman who becomes a bandit. He is a romantic man of mystery, eyes blazing, hat pulled down, sword drawn, as he steps from nowhere. He has an uncertain past and a fatal future. He is a man of destiny who sets events into motion.

Hernani loves Doña Sol, Don Ruy Gomez's ward and fiancée, and furtively meets her at great risk. Don Carlos, the Spanish king, is also in love with her, and after forcing his way into her room one night he hides in a closet and listens to her conversation with Hernani. Doña Sol prepares to elope with Hernani to his mountain-retreat, when Don Carlos intervenes. But Don Ruy Gomez arrives and Hernani manages to escape in the confusion.

Unaware of Don Carlos' ambush Hernani returns for Doña Sol, though after a long mental struggle he decides not to expose her to the dangers that await him in the mountains. He fights Don Carlos but refuses to kill him because the King will not bear arms against an inferior. Hernani is galled because he has sworn to avenge his father, whom the Spanish monarch unjustly executed. Once more Hernani escapes.

He returns disguised as a pilgrim to Don Gomez's ancestral home. Don Carlos arrives with a retinue to seize him, but without knowing Hernani's identity Don Gomez obeys the chivalrous code to protect his guests. He hides the stranger. Then he harangues the King about honor before the ancestral portraits of the House of Gomez. But Don Carlos unheedingly kidnaps Doña Sol, and after emerging from his hiding-place Hernani is angered to learn what has happened. Filled with gratitude for Don Gomez's protection, he promises to give his life in repayment whenever the Duke wishes.

Hernani plots with other conspirators to kill Don Carlos during the election for the Emperor of the Holy Roman Empire. They await him in Charlemagne's tomb, where the King undergoes a metamorphosis in character. The attempted assassination fails, but Don Carlos, the newly elected Emperor, forgives the conspirators and graciously allows Hernani and Doña Sol to marry.

Don Gomez, once his ward's fiancé, is insanely jealous. After Hernani and his bride leave the wedding-feast, he blows his horn. Hernani knows that he must die because he has given his word as a Spanish nobleman. Despite his protest he cannot reconcile Don Gomez. He drinks the poison, and when Doña Sol, his grief-stricken bride, follows suit Don Gomez stabs himself in grief.

Balzac's Louis Lambert is a genius whom society misunderstands and persecutes. Born of destitute tanners, little Louis is sent as a child to an uncle, a curate in Mer, for supervision and study. There Mme de Staël comes across him by chance and immediately recognizes his budding genius. She subsidizes him in school at Vendôme, where he becomes a mathematician and philosopher although the school regards him as a poor student. His schoolmates nickname him Pythagoras, and he has only one friend—the narrator of the novel. Both faculty and students mock him because they are in fact jealous of him. They rejoice when it becomes evident that Mme de Staël has forgotten her protégé. Young Pythagoras becomes the campus scapegoat.

Louis is a small, delicate boy who lives in his imagination. At twelve, for instance, he relives the holocaust at Austerlitz by reading a description of the battle. While in school he writes a *Traité de la volonté,* which his professors destroy upon discovery. His imagination is his only consolation.

His imagination is also destructive. Lambert accepts a Swedenborgian notion of the universe in which every man possesses angelic potentiality. But he must cultivate his spirit to the exclusion of the world if he is to fulfill his celestial calling. Otherwise the angelic element dies in a process of materialization, and man becomes a purely material thing. Like Swedenborg, Lambert believes that man must nourish his spirit so that it will be prepared to assume the functions of the higher life which he enters through death. As he cultivates his inner life Lambert turns increasingly away from the world. His introspection results in the breakdown of his ability to communicate, but it is uncertain whether he is in fact mad.

After school at Vendôme Lambert spends some time with his uncle, the curate, and leaves for Paris to see Mme de Staël. He arrives just as she is dying. A desultory experience in the business world follows; then he returns to Blois, where he falls in love with Pauline de Villenoix. What seems a psychotic break prevents their marriage. He alternates between "madness" and lucidity for the remainder of his life,

and he emasculates himself during an insane seizure. He no
longer communicates with anyone, even Pauline, though she
jots down his disconnected observations on life, death, the
soul, during his increasingly rare moments of lucidity. These
fragments comprise his message on Swedenborgianism. Lambert dies in 1824 on the eve of his marriage to Pauline.

These romantic heroes are essentially similar.

It is evident from these character sketches that the romantic hero plays several roles. He is a poet-prophet, man of
sensibility, psychopath, solitary, wanderer, criminal, rebel,
seeker, prototype of the Messiah. He is the fatal man, the pale
genius, the ostracized magus, the victim of fate. For instance,
René is a seeker, wanderer, fatal man. Hernani is a fatal
man and rebel. Lambert is a poet-prophet and pathological
hero. It is indeed difficult to classify any romantic hero into
one neat category since the roles most often overlap.

But it seems that whatever role he *might* play, the romantic hero is immediately recognizable because he is always
self-consciously unique. He is convinced there has never been
another like him, and he feels superior because he is in fact
exceptional. He is always a titan because his happiness and
sorrow always exceed the emotional capacity of an ordinary
man. The hero is transfigured through his romantic sensi-
bililty, i.e., his peculiar pattern of emotional response and
sensory perception. Self-awareness together with romantic
sensibility, moreover, equals the romantic self-consciousness.
The romantic hero is the self-conscious hero.

Self-consciousness distinguishes the romantic hero from
earlier hero-types. Whereas for example the classic ideal man
controls his emotions by reason, the romantic hero is not
bound by reason but rather follows the bent of his sensibility.[16] The classic ideal man, in short,[17]

. . . views the mere stimulation of emotional excitement and
the unschooled liberation of impulses as at best a temporary
narcotic, the awakening from which inevitably brings in its
train . . . a dichotomy of mind and feeling, and a dissatisfaction

based not so much on intellectual conviction as on mere insecurity of feeling.

Such an ideal man assumes that emotion interferes with accurate perception, but the romantic hero believes that sensibility heightens his cognitive powers. Thus the hero's aim is justified, although his sensibility may ultimately result in the exaggerated forms of hypersensibility or even in overt pathology.

Self-consciousness is the common denominator of men like René, Hernani, and Lambert. It may therefore be hypothesized that the romantic hero belongs essentially to one hero-type, who may assume different roles, rather than to a series of romantic heroes. He reveals himself in his different roles while still remaining in each instance the self-conscious hero.

The hypothesis that the romantic hero is the self-conscious hero may be expanded by establishing two fundamental propositions. First, the romantic hero feels that he is unique. Second, he believes that each man is different from every other man. The various manifestations of the hero-type result from these two propositions and are subsumed by the tenet that the romantic hero is the self-conscious hero.

First, the romantic hero is in fact unique. He feels essentially different from other men and cannot appreciably identify his aims and emotions with theirs. Now he may differ from ordinary men in one of two ways: He must be either better or worse, either superior or inferior. Comparison cannot be avoided. It is a matter of fact that the hero considers himself superior to the herdman.

Second, each man is different from every other man in the romantic worldview. Just as there are no two identical sets of fingerprints, there are no two identical men. There is always a different focus which distinguishes one from another. Admittedly the degree of difference is much smaller between two herdmen than between a herdman and the hero. In acknowledging such a difference the classicist emphasizes the essential likeness of men while the romantic emphasizes the basic difference.

It now remains to account hypothetically for the variations in the romantic hero-role. It seems that the archetypal self-conscious hero becomes a particular kind of romantic hero by responding differently to a given situation. A study of romantic literature warrants an investigation of the hypothesis that the romantic hero as self-conscious hero assumes one or more of five roles or a pseudo-role. He is a seeker, a man of fate, a pathological hero, a poet-prophet, or a rebel. In his pseudo-role the protagonist is the anti-hero, i.e., the man who comments wryly upon his own failure to achieve heroism. These roles are the principal lines of descent from the all-inclusive archetype, the self-conscious hero.

III

This study expands the concept that the romantic hero is actually a manifestation of an archetypal self-conscious hero. The different roles which the self-conscious hero assumes are the subject of the individual chapters. The primary sources for this work are the appropriate works of Chateaubriand, Constant, Sénancour, Lamartine, Vigny, Musset, Hugo, Balzac, Dumas *père*, Stendhal, Barbey d'Aurevilly, Nerval, and Baudelaire, or from the appearance of *Le Génie du christianisme* in 1802 to *Les Fleurs du mal* in 1857. The men and dates are not so arbitrary as they may seem since romanticism is not a literature which exists in France between 1820 and 1843. It is rather a movement characterized by certain fundamental changes in worldview, and it is unjustifiable to omit Chateaubriand as pre-romantic or Baudelaire as transitional. Such writers have been included because their protagonists are often prime examples of the romantic hero.

This is a philosophical rather than an exhaustive survey of the romantic hero's appearance in French literature. Principles are of course the primary concern, and illustrations are valuable primarily as they embody principles. Our purpose is to establish who the romantic hero really is and to investigate the forces which mold him. Perhaps France is more fruitful as a subject than any other European nation. For here the social and philosophical forces shaping the romantic worldview contrast most sharply with the pre-Revolutionary period, and the romantic hero himself is most clearly embodied. In France he is seen in his pristine form.

ONE

THE SEEKER

SINCE every hero is a seeker who explicitly or implicitly is looking for something, the romantic hero is engaged in a quest like any other hero-type. But the romantic quest differs from other goals by a peculiar dichotomy of reality-ideality of which the hero is self-consciously aware. In this context self-consciousness involves both self-awareness and romantic sensibility, and it works in the following way. His sharp, critical self-awareness causes acute dissatisfaction with mundane reality, and his romantic sensibility impels him forward in a search for ideality. This split between reality and ideality characterizes the romantic seeker.

There are three main aspects to the romantic quest, i.e., the search for the meaning of self and ideality. First, the hero may be a wanderer who actually travels throughout the world in search of the absolute and the infinite. Second, he may be a thinker who regards knowledge either as an absolute which leads him to the infinite or as a relative through which he approaches the absolute. Third, he may be a mystic who discovers ideality by transcending reality. The idea of the mystic subsumes the deathwish since the hero discovers ideality in death as he passes from worldly reality to infinity,

15

from nothingness to being. Yet in each case the hero remains a seeker characterized by his self-conscious search for ideality. This classification of the seeker can be justified by examining several heroes.

THE WANDERER

René is impelled in the romantic quest by the *mal du siècle* from which he suffers. In the volcano image he describes the ennui and emotional turmoil which victimize him and in fact cause him to become a wanderer:[1]

Un jeune homme, plein de passions, assis sur la bouche d'un volcan, et pleurant sur les mortels dont à peine il voyoit à ses pieds les demeures, n'est sans doute, ô vieillards, qu'un objet digne de votre pitié; mais, quoi que vous puissiez penser de René, ce tableau vous offre l'image de son caractère et de son existence: c'est ainsi que toute ma vie j'ai eu devant les yeux une création à la fois immense et imperceptible, et un abîme ouvert à mes côtés.

The volcano is actually the hypersensibility which René cannot harness. Dissatisfied with society, he turns first to ancient civilizations and then to the New World in his search for ideality. He expresses his nervous energy in the quest. He believes that ideality exists as an ideal state of reality, e.g., the perfect society, and that he will find peace when he discovers utopia.

His salvation rests upon finding El Dorado, the perfect society. He is desperate because his quest in Europe has been fruitless; neither ancient ruins nor modern cities give meaning to his life:[2]

. . . Qu'avois-je appris jusqu'alors avec tant de fatigue? Rien de certain parmi les anciens, rien de beau parmi les modernes. Le passé et le présent sont deux statues incomplètes: l'une a été retirée toute mutilée du débris des âges; l'autre n'a pas encore reçu sa perfection de l'avenir.

If perfection cannot be recaptured from the past and if it cannot be realized in modern Europe, then it must lie elsewhere if it exists at all. Hence René turns to the New World in his search:[3]

Je recherchai surtout dans mes voyages les artistes et ces hommes divins qui chantent les Dieux sur la lyre, et la félicité des peuples qui honorent les loix, la religion et les tombeaux.

And if such people exist they must inhabit the New World. The ideal man is the noble savage, and the perfect society is the American Indian tribe.

Despair and hypersensibility impel him on this voyage to America. René characterizes himself as he says:[4]

Levez-vous vite, orages désirés, qui devez emporter René dans les espaces d'une autre vie! Ainsi disant, je marchois à grands pas, le visage enflammé, le vent sifflant dans ma chevelure, ne sentant ni pluie, ni frimas, enchanté, tourmenté, et comme possédé par le démon de mon coeur.

But René destroys himself like a storm spending its own fury. He finds that ideality is elusive. The noble savage enjoys the fruits of an ideal society without suffering the agony of the romantic quest, while René, who searches and suffers so long, cannot enjoy his Indian utopia. He apostrophizes the noble savage by way of explanation:[5]

Heureux sauvages! Oh! que ne puis-je jouir de la paix qui vous accompagne toujours! Tandis qu'avec si peu de fruit je parcourois tant de contrées, vous, assis tranquillement sous vos chênes, vous laissiez couler les jours sans les compter. Votre raison n'étoit que vos besoins, et vous arriviez, mieux que moi, au résultat de la sagesse, comme l'enfant, entre les jeux et le sommeil.

For René cannot seize the spirit of the noble savage by adopting his dress and manners. René remains the tempestuous hero who cannot enter the utopia where his wanderings lead him. He suffers like Tantalus for the ideality he seeks eludes him.

Chactas, a wise old Indian, observes that René must indeed remain himself, i.e., what he is rather than what he wants to be:[6]

O le plus vénérable des Sachems, chaste et pure hermine des

vieux chênes, que ne puis-je t'emmener dans mes forêts! Mais je
le sens, tu n'es pas fait pour habiter parmi des Sauvages. . . .

He realizes that René is a child of European culture and cannot really become an Indian. René's quest is doomed from
the beginning because he is unable to change. He remains
the self which he despises, from which he flees, but from
which he cannot escape. In short René as a seeker cannot
step from reality, which repulses him, into ideality, which
eludes him. Thus his quest results in profound disillusionment and ennui.

René wants too much. He is reckless while pursuing the
quest, and to the extent that he as a seeker is also a fatal man,
he destroys others. In *Les Natchez*, for example, he notes that
he is caught in a typical impasse:[7]

René connut presque à la fois le jugement qui le condamnoit à
sortir de la Louisiane, et l'ordre de l'exécution immédiate de ce
jugement. Cet homme, étranger sur ce globe, cherchoit en vain
un coin de terre où il pût reposer sa tête: partout où il s'étoit
montré, il avoit créé des misères. Que retrouveroit-il en Europe?
une femme malheureuse. Que laisseroit-il en Amérique? une
femme malheureuse.

René defeats himself through his *vague des passions*,[8] i.e., his
hypersensibility, just as he is fatal to others. He explains the
cause of his failure to Céluta, his Indian wife:[9]

Je suppose, Céluta, que le coeur de René s'ouvre maintenant
devant toi: vois-tu le monde extraordinaire qu'il renferme? il
sort de ce coeur des flammes qui manquent d'aliment, qui dévoreraient la création sans être rassasiées, qui te dévoreraient toi-
même. Prends garde, femme de vertu! recule devant cet abîme:
laisse-le dans mon sein! Père tout-puissant, tu m'as appelé dans
la solitude; tu m'as dit "René! René! Qu'as-tu fait de ta soeur?"
Suis-je donc Caïn?

Ironically his hypersensibility, while impelling him on the
romantic quest, prevents him from achieving his goal of
ideality. For through his nervous disposition René can never
participate in the utopia which he as a wanderer finds with
the American Indians.

The relationship between the romantic writer and his hero should be clarified. Usually they cannot be separated; the writer is in fact his hero. For instance, Chateaubriand projects his own quest as a seeker into his fictional counterpart. Like René he knows that the impetus for the quest, i.e., his imagination and sensibility, is also responsible for his failure. And he poses a question which applies to René as well as to himself:[10]

Que faisait à cela mon élégante démone? Par sa magie, elle me transportait au bord du Nil, me montrait la pyramide égyptienne noyée dans le sable, comme un jour le sillon armoricain caché sous la bruyère: je m'applaudissais d'avoir placé les fables de ma félicité hors du cercle des réalités humaines.

Sensibility spurs him *à la découverte du monde*,[11] but it is destructive since Chateaubriand, again like René, cannot harness and focus his energy. Both author and romantic hero are caught between two centuries "comme au confluent de deux fleuves,"[12] and they respond hypersensitively to the passing of the old values and the birth of the new. This hypersensitivity, uncontrolled and undirected, prevents them from realizing the new values represented by the quest. Chateaubriand as a wanderer externalizes his search and asks:[13]

Je n'emportais que ma jeunesse et mes illusions; je désertais un monde dont j'avais foulé la poussière et compté les étoiles, pour un monde de qui la terre et le ciel m'étaient inconnus. Que devait-il m'arriver si j'atteignais le but de mon voyage?

In these lines he establishes the dichotomy reality-ideality, but he does not intimate whether he realizes his aim. But his romantic hero, René, realizes the external goal of the quest by finding a utopia. Yet René's discovery is unsatisfactory as he learns at last that ideality is a state of mind rather than an external state of being, and his hypersensibility does not permit him to enjoy the tranquillity of this state of mind.

Obermann, or Superman, is another wanderer. In the romantic quest he seeks to know ideality through flashes of intuition. He does not conceive ideality externally like René.

As a wanderer Obermann travels in pursuit of sensations from which he will later attempt a recreation of ideality. Nature is his raw material.

Sénancour's *Obermann* has no plot-structure; it is primarily the record of spots of time when the hero's heightened sensations afford an insight into the essence of reality. Moreover such essence is ideality. For in the study of his own impressions Obermann is increasingly liberated from reality conceived as mere sense-impression, and he accordingly participates more and more in nature, the universe, infinity. Béguin observes in this connection:[14]

Devenir soi-même ce que veut l'ambiance, s'y confondre et se laisser modeler d'instant en instant, cette extase toute passive tend à une sorte d'anéantissement de la réalité extérieure par elle-même. L'état de bonheur auquel aspire le rêveur à ces moments-là est celui d'une existence arrachée aux sensations par l'accumulation même des sensations. La réalité visible, lorsqu'on s'y mêle et s'y identifie, finit par se transfigurer; au lieu de la perception banale qui la considère comme un objet extérieur au moi, on atteint à cette autre appréhension qui ne fait plus de différence entre le sentiment interne et les choses perçues hors du moi.

Since ideality is a state of mind, the hero pursues the quest by searching the recesses of his mind. The subject and the object have a peculiar relation as a result of the romantic sensibility. For example, he explains the relationship of a particular sensation to infinity or ideality in the following way:[15]

Ce que peut avoir de séduisant la multitude de rapports qui lient chaque individu à son espèce et à l'univers, cette attente expansive que donne à un coeur jeune tout un monde à expérimenter, ce dehors inconnu et fantastique, ce prestige est décoloré, fugitif, évanoui. Ce monde terrestre offert à l'action de mon être est devenu aride et nu: j'y cherchais la vie de l'âme, il ne la contient pas.

Obermann looks within himself as a seeker in his effort to

interpret the sense-impressions which he gathers on his quest.
He explains his role as the wanderer:[16]

Mais il faut . . . que je cherche, que je me hâte vers l'inconnu,
et que, sans savoir où je vais, je fuie le présent comme si j'avais
quelque espoir dans l'avenir.

Both self-awareness and romantic sensibility are motivating
factors in the quest. Obermann states, first, that he is conscious of his predicament and, second, that a force impels
him on the quest. Thus his search for the unknown is self-
consciously desperate. Life is short, each instant precious,
and the memory must cherish the sense-impression until its
meaning bears fruit and becomes apparent. Death comes so
soon:[17]

Que veux-je? Espérer, puis n'espérer plus, c'est être ou n'être
plus: voilà l'homme, sans doute. Mais comment se fait-il qu'après
les chants d'une voix émue, après les parfums des fleurs, et les
soupirs de l'imagination, et les élans de la pensée, il faille mourir?

Conscious of human mortality, Obermann races time while
engaged on the quest. As a seeker he wants to resolve the
basic riddle of man's existence:[18]

De l'Homme fatigué d'avidité et accablé de foiblesse. Da sa vie
sans borne et sans résultat, puissante au dehors, et misérable au
dedans, nulle dans l'univers, et incompréhensible sur la terre.

And nature is the raw material from which he gleans the
impressions necessary for a glimpse into ideality, i.e., the
essence of reality. His quest is more cerebral than René's.
Whereas he identifies ideality with an ideal state of reality,
Obermann is invariably concerned with a state of mind. In
this respect he begins with a notion of ideality which René
gains only after a lifetime as a wanderer.

Obermann's concept of ideality is metaphysical rather than
mystical. Whereas the seeker as mystic looks, for example,
upon death as reincorporation into the infinite, Obermann
believes that it is simply the cessation of life; it regrettably
makes further pursuit of the quest impossible. Even worse,
death is a temptation since it sways man from his basic aim

in life—the pursuit of the quest. Consequently the deathwish becomes a mode of evasion, of escape:[19]

Cependant je suis plus calme maintenant, et je commence à me lasser de mon impatience même. Des idées sombres, mais tranquilles, me deviennent plus familières. Je songe volontiers à ceux qui, le matin de leurs jours, ont trouvé leur éternelle nuit; ce sentiment me repose et me console, c'est l'instinct du soir. Mais pourquoi ce besoin des ténèbres? pourquoi la lumière m'est-elle pénible? Ils le sauront un jour; quand ils auront changé, quand je ne serai plus.

Death is an appealing avenue of escape, and the deathwish results from the seeker's despair of discovering ideality. Suicide tempts him during his moments of anguish:[20]

Dès longtemps la vie me fatigue. . . . Je trouve aussi quelque répugnance à perdre irrévocablement mon être. S'il fallait choisir à l'instant, ou de briser tous les liens, ou d'y rester nécessairement attaché pendant quarante ans encore, je crois que j'hésiterais peu; mais je me hâte moins, parce que dans quelques mois je le pourrai comme aujourd'hui, et que les Alpes sont le seul lieu qui convienne à la manière dont je voudrais m'éteindre.

There is no religious motif in his concept of death as there is, for example, in Nerval's. Death is simply a temptation, born of despair, to which he must not yield. However difficult the quest, Obermann believes the wanderer must push on, sometimes blindly, often meaningfully, just as in his despair he turns to the mountains of self-knowledge which represent at once his deathwish and a haven of rest in the quest for ideality.

THE THINKER

The romantic hero may follow another path to ideality. He may conceive of the mind as his world and traverse the realm of thought. This is not to say, however, that the hero as thinker takes no cognizance of objective reality; the contrary is indeed the case. He is related to the world as subject to object, and he is self-consciously rational. The seeker uses his intellect in the pursuit of the romantic quest, the goal of which is still ideality.

Vigny exemplifies the seeker as thinker. He believes that man can find ideality through thought; that is, he can effect an ideal state of reality through human understanding. The hero is of course an idealist since he believes that rationality can effect such progress. It is certainly erroneous to see only pessimism in Vigny because his belief in progress is distinctly idealistic.

Vigny's idealism motivates him to formulate a concept of ideality. Consider for instance his idea of honor through which a new, higher society is born. Then ideality becomes a possibility which the hero as a rational being may very well realize. In *Servitude et grandeur militaires* Vigny recounts his experiences with the French army in an effort to formulate a system of values for such an ideal possibility. Honor undergirds the system as the archstone by which men, acting in concord, can effect an earthly ideality. Castex observes in this connection:[21]

. . . Il s'élève au dessus de toutes les considérations particulières pour définir en termes solennels la religion de l'honneur. . . . Jamais Vigny ne s'est élevé plus haut que dans cet ultime chapitre où, s'affranchissant de son pessimisme, il découvre une nouvelle justification de l'existence pour l'homme inquiet des temps modernes.

Indeed Vigny elevates honor into a religion in the following rhapsody:[22]

Gardons-nous de dire de ce dieu antique de l'Honneur que c'est un faux dieu, car la pierre de son autel est peut-être celle du Dieu inconnu. L'aimant magique de cette pierre attire et attache les coeurs d'acier, le coeur des forts.—Dites si cela n'est pas, vous, mes braves Compagnons, vous à qui j'ai fait ces récits, ô nouvelle légion Thébaine, vous dont la tête se fit écraser sur cette pierre du Serment, dites-le, vous tous, Saints et Martyrs de la religion de L'HONNEUR.

But honor as an ideal is impotent unless there is a force strong enough to realize it. Such a force is rationality; man can use his mind as the instrument of ideality. To Vigny the French army at its best exemplifies the effect of honor, and it also shows the relation of idealism to ideality. For when a group like the French army, as a microcosm of society, bases its code upon honor, then idealism results in meaningful action and such action in the realization of ideality. But idealism alone, without action, is always ineffective.

Vigny always identifies ideality with man's realizable aspirations, however high they may be. Ideality is an ideal possibility—any perfect state rather than one particular state of being. In short he does not prescribe a specific utopia. In "La Bouteille à la mer," for example, he conceives of ideality in terms of man ameliorating his lot through the painful advance of scientific knowledge. In "La Maison du berger" he visualizes ideality as the perfect love. In "Moïse" it is the potentiality of the Ten Commandments as a moral code. And in other works he envisions different facets of man's great potentiality.

It is evident that Vigny is most often empirical. He tends to regard the religious or mystical quest as illusory; hence his concept of ideality is vague whenever he introduces the mystical or religious motif. Faguet observes in this respect:[23]

Le vrai tourment du mélancolique qui est d'adorer l'idéal et de n'y pas croire, nul ne l'a si pleinement connu que lui, ni si constamment. Il lui était également impossible et de ne pas aimer la gloire, l'amour, le bonheur, la religion, et de croire à la gloire, à l'amour, au bonheur et à Dieu.

This judgment must be qualified because Vigny separates absolute from contingent goals. As an empiricist he cannot subscribe to abstract goals; he has no eternal panaceas for the world and delineates no immutable utopia for mankind. He is too realistic to think other than concretely, even though he postulates ideal states of being. As a seeker Vigny may indeed long for absolute certainty, but as a thinker he settles for contingency in the quest. He conceives life as an ever-enlarging circle of ideal possibilities, each of which leads into another. The present state of science would exemplify an ideal possibility to the Captain in "La Bouteille à la mer," but the modern scientist is dissatisfied with such achievement because he is aware of even greater potentiality. One circle leads into another, just as the Captain is responsible for contemporary science, just as modern science will produce future developments. Ideality is the horizon, elusive but always visible. In brief Vigny believes that ideality is contingent. It is potentiality, i.e., the ideal possibility. Otherwise he would be a mystic or a wanderer rather than a thinker. As it is, however, Vigny relies upon human reason, and he says that the hero's task as thinker is to show man how he can effect an ideal possibililty by using his divine reason.

THE MYSTIC

The mystic also identifies the romantic quest with the pursuit of knowledge. But whereas the thinker rationally approaches knowledge and ideality, the mystic is of course suprarational. He believes that to see into ideality he must supersede reason, which he regards as too finite to approach the absolute and the infinite. The question arises at this point whether or not the romantic hero is a true mystic, for there seems to be a basic confusion between the mystic and the mysterious. This is no place for a lengthy discussion of mysticism. It is nevertheless true that the romantic mystic generally attempts to absorb reality into himself whereas earlier mystics usually seek to incorporate themselves into reality. Perhaps the question hinges upon a notion of the romantic ego and is best answered in terms of the mystic as a self-conscious hero. First, he is aware that reason does not suffice to know reality; his intellectual position, then, precludes rationality as a mode of knowing the essence of reality, i.e., ideality. Second, he believes that knowledge, i.e., insight, is spontaneous and intuitive; he does not rationally understand the Word though he perceives it. Moreover the romantic mystic knows that he has such insight because he is preoccupied with the Word and because he is attuned to the nature of things. His hypersensitivity enables him to comprehend ideality, and his understanding is fundamentally suprarational. Examples amplify this point.

Gérard de Nerval is obsessed with the infinite and the absolute. As a seeker he turns to esotericism and the study of comparative religion in his quest for truth. Myths recur in his poetry and prose while he frequently steps beyond the tenuous line of reality into the dreamlife. His poems and stories record his pursuit of the quest and evidence his "passion pour les études ésotériques."[24] Jeanine Moulin observes:[25]

Une scrupuleuse lecture révèle bientôt les constantes de sa pensée et de ses sentiments: formation d'un idéal mystico-amoureux et d'un syncrétisme religieux, tentative d'assurer l'éternité de son âme. Elles se joignent à travers ses vers et sa prose, fil conducteur, parfois détourné, jamais rompu.

It is the pattern of religious experience rather than the individual experience itself which Nerval finds meaningful. Intellectually he surveys and compares the varieties of religious expression, and he derives an intuitive, suprarational understanding of the pattern. Moulin points out that in "Delfica" and "Myrtho" Nerval illustrates how[26]

le christianisme avait absorbé le paganisme sans le détruire; un nouveau paganisme se préparait sous le nom de "libre-pensée," lequel, à son tour, absorberait le christianisme sans le détruire. Cette théorie court tout au long des écrits des Illuminés; Gérard considérait les Templiers du Moyen-âge, les secrets modernes des Rose-croix, et les francs-maçons, comme des formes rajeunies des antiques cultes d'initiés.

One religion absorbs another while the basic pattern of religious experience remains the same in all religions.

Now the mystic may be concerned with the historical pattern of such experience, but Nerval believes that the meaning of the pattern cannot be logically derived. The mystic perceives the meaning, the Word, immediately and intuitively. He is suprarational. Ideality, i.e., the perception of the Word, is the meaning of the pattern which exists as an absolute in the temporal continuity of specific manifestations. By deriving higher truth from the pattern—ideality—Nerval is a mystic pursuing the romantic quest.

There is no incompatibility between Nerval's mysticism, his study of comparative religion, and his obsession with the dreamlife. They are simply different avenues of the quest and do not exclude one another; both mysticism and religion appear for example in "l'épanchement du songe dans la vie."[27] The hallucination and the dream guide Nerval in his quest, for they too contain the pattern of experience from which he mystically abstracts truth.

The deathwish is a key theme in his mystic concept of ideality. Death is a religious experience which symbolizes the reincorporation of man into infinity; consequently the deathwish plays an important role in the quest. After attempting suicide Nerval writes in *Octavie:*[28]

Mourir, grand Dieu! pourquoi cette idée me revient-elle à tout propos, comme s'il n'y avait que ma mort qui fût l'équivalent du bonheur que vous promettez? La mort! ce mot ne répand cependant rien de sombre dans ma pensée. Elle m'apparaît couronnée de roses pâles, comme à la fin d'un festin; j'ai rêvé quelquefois qu'elle m'attendait en souriant au chevet d'une femme adorée, après le bonheur, après l'ivresse, et qu'elle me disait: "Allons, jeune homme! tu as eu toute ta part de joie en ce monde. A présent, viens dormir, viens te reposer dans mes bras. Je ne suis pas belle, moi, mais je suis bonne et secourable, et je ne donne pas le plaisir, mais le calme éternel."

His attitude towards death is ambivalent in this passage. First, death tempts the seeker from pursuing the quest; in this sense it is a retreat from ideality. Second, death is a mystical experience and point of departure in the quest of ideality rather than the terminus of life. Not only is Nerval's attitude ambivalent, but his concept of death is also ambiguous. Antipodal attitudes characterize him at different times. But as the quietus of life's agony or the gateway to the infinite and absolute, the deathwish exerts a temptation which Nerval resists only with difficulty and to which he finally succumbs in fact by hanging himself. In spite of pathological overtones the deathwish, for the most part, manifests the mystico-religious aspect of the romantic quest. The seeker finds in death an entrance to the realm of ideality. After all, such has been the belief of most great religions. Nerval as a mystic is testifying to his own faith in the higher reality.

The mystic side to Baudelaire as seeker is reflected in "Le Voyage," "L'Invitation au voyage," and "Bohémiens en voyage." In each poem he externalizes the romantic quest by making a wanderer of the seeking hero. The wanderer may search for the infinite and the absolute like the gipsies of "Bohémiens en voyage" with no specific ideal in mind, their quest springing from an irritating malaise. Or he may proceed towards a definite goal equated with death, for Baudelaire, like Nerval, thinks death is the entrance to ideality.

The wanderer begins his quest as a child fascinated by the mysterious world at his fingertips in prints and maps. His first voyages are a child's fantasies. Later he embarks on the quest, a cosmic voyage, which does not necessarily have an actual counterpart:[29]

> Mais les vrais voyageurs sont ceux-là seuls qui partent
> Pour partir; coeurs légers, semblables aux ballons,
> De leur fatalité jamais ils ne s'écartent,
> Et, sans savoir pourquoi, disent toujours: Allons!
>
> Ceux-là dont les désirs ont la forme des nues,
> Et qui rêvent, ainsi qu'un conscrit le canon,
> De vastes voluptés, changeantes, inconnues,
> Et dont l'esprit humain n'a jamais su le nom!

The adult pursues the adolescent's quest and gives new meaning to his dream. The concrete world of ideality, as it exists in the child's imagination, is metamorphosed. It becomes chimerical and the quest comes increasingly to victimize the wanderer:[30]

> O le pauvre amoureux des pays chimériques!
> Faut-il le mettre aux fers, le jeter à la mer,
> Ce matelot ivrogne, inventeur d'Amériques
> Dont le mirage rend le gouffre plus amer?

Both as adolescent and adult the wanderer loves an illusion and is agonized for and by his dreams. For the quest, which must be pursued, consumes the wanderer:[31]

> Faut-il partir? rester? Si tu peux rester, reste;
> Pars, s'il le faut. L'un court, et l'autre se tapit

Pour tromper l'ennemi vigilant et funeste,
Le Temps! Il est, hélas! des coureurs sans répit,

Comme le Juif errant et comme les apôtres,
A qui rien ne suffit, ni wagon, ni vaisseau,
Pour fuir ce rétiaire infâme; il en est d'autres
Qui savent le tuer sans quitter leur berceau.

The gipsy is a type of the wanderer who has no real choice
on the quest; he wanders through the world because it is his
nature to do so. And the quest exercises an irresistible appeal
for the mystic as for the gipsies of "Bohémiens en voyage":[32]

Du fond de son réduit sablonneux, le grillon,
Les regardant passer, redouble sa chanson;
Cybèle, qui les aime, augmente ses verdures,

Fait couler le rocher et fleurir le désert!
Devant ces voyageurs, pour lesquels est ouvert
L'empire familier des ténèbres futures.

The wanderer seeks a utopia, an ideal realm which Baudelaire visualizes in "L'Invitation au voyage":[33]

Mon enfant, ma soeur,
Songe à la douceur
D'aller là-bas vivre ensemble!
Aimer à loisir,
Aimer et mourir
Au pays qui te ressemble!
Les soleils mouillés
De ces ciels brouillés
Pour mon esprit ont les charmes
Si mystérieux
De tes traîtres yeux,
Brillant à travers leurs larmes.

Là, tout n'est qu'ordre et beauté,
Luxe, calme et volupté.

But these tranquil, luxurious visions are not the ultimate
ideality. They are simply figures of the infinite and the absolute—a concrete image of what the wanderer might hope to

find at the end of his quest. But ideality itself, antipodal to the drab reality which victimizes the poet, remains elusive—a cosmic concept rather than an actual oasis in the desert.

Perhaps Baudelaire means that ideality is too much for the seeker to grasp. He longs for it, he knows he cannot find it, and he suffers. Poetry and religion are at once his consolation and mode of approaching ideality as closely as earth allows. The poet sees the essence of reality just as the man of God glimpses the infinite. But in their role as mystic both poet and man of God never have a pure vision of ideality like the mystic Nerval.

The romantic quest leads inexorably to death, which is again an avenue of escape at the same time it is a gate to the infinite. Baudelaire voices his deathwish in "Le Voyage":[34]

> O Mort, vieux capitaine, il est temps! levons l'ancre!
> Ce pays nous ennuie, ô Mort! Appareillons!
> Si le ciel et la mer sont noirs comme de l'encre,
> Nos coeurs que tu connais sont remplis de rayons!
>
> Verse-nous ton poison pour qu'il nous réconforte!
> Nous voulons, tant ce feu nous brûle le cerveau,
> Plonger au fond du gouffre, Enfer ou Ciel, qu'importe?
> Au fond de l'Inconnu pour trouver du *nouveau!*

Thus the deathwish tempts the seeker from while simultaneously impelling him in the romantic quest. After all, the goal is the same—the cessation of the agony of life—and death is the great release. The seeker is ultimately freed of his limitations in the realm of ideality through the mystical experience of death.

SUMMARY

The seeker is concerned with the dichotomy ideality-reality in the romantic quest. Moreover he is self-consciously engaged in this quest. His acute awareness of life makes reality seem repugnant, and his hypersensibility drives him in his search for ideality. This ideality he seeks for in one or more of three ways. He looks for an ideal state of reality, he attempts to effect an ideal potentiality, or he seeks to know ideality through the mystical experience. In other words he may be a wanderer, a thinker, or a mystic; but in each case he remains the seeker, the self-conscious hero. The lines separating these three classes are sometimes tenuous, but the broad categories nevertheless emerge and present the seeker in his romantic role.

TWO

THE MAN OF FATE

There are two basic aspects of the romantic hero as a man of fate. First, he is a fated man when his character progresses towards a predetermined end in a given context. As a fated hero his actions may be predetermined by himself, the social context, or cosmic forces, but in each instance he acts according to a romantic concept of inevitability which destroys all resistance. Second, the romantic hero is a fatal man when he acts destructively. In this role he may wittingly or unwillingly destroy others, or his relationship with them somehow causes them to destroy themselves. The idea of necessity is again paramount. The man of fate may be at once both a fated man and a fatal man, although one aspect tends to dominate the other.

Perhaps some idea of necessity applies to any hero since obviously he reacts to forces over which he has limited control in any context. The difference between such an idea of necessity and the romantic concept of fatality is of course one of degree, but there is an even more important distinction—the nature of the romantic hero. In the concept of fatality the romantic hero differs from other hero-types by his self-conscious awareness of the role he plays as a man of fate in society and the universe. Here as elsewhere self-consciousness includes both awareness and the romantic sensibility. Unlike the Greek tragic hero, for instance, the romantic hero is profoundly aware of himself in his role; he is a cerebral hero who watches himself struggle in the mesh of fate. His romantic sensibility either promotes or motivates the struggle; in other words, the hero's reaction intensifies the struggle in his peculiar relation to fate. In this way the romantic hero as the man of fate is unique.

It is possible to study the man of fate separately as the fatal man or the fated man. But since the roles usually overlap, it is best to examine him from both standpoints at once. This method allows a closer organization of material on a hero rather than distributing it within two sections. For example, René will be considered in one section rather than two. Furthermore, this method avoids artificial distinctions as much as possible. Usually the fatal man and the fated man are too closely related for one to be studied apart from the other. For this reason the term "man of fate" has been chosen to describe what is most often the dual aspect of the same romantic hero.

THE SOCIAL CONTEXT

The man of fate is an instrument of necessity in the social context. As such he may be an executor of fatality who sets into motion a concatenation of events which destroy others, or he may in turn be victimized since certain causes in society effect his own end. Usually he is both at once. There is however a variety of response, since the fated man's actions may be predetermined by forces he cannot control or he may indeed accelerate his own catastrophe. The matter is subtle and complicated. As men of fate the poet and the man of sensibility most clearly illustrate the problem in the social context.

The poet is a man of fate because both gods and men envy and destroy the genius. To a certain extent this notion derives from antiquity, but Estève summarizes the way in which the classical notion is fundamentally different from the romantic concept:[1]

Cette idée que le génie est un don fatal est aussi vieille que la littérature. Mais les poètes classiques donnaient du fait l'explication la plus simple: toute grandeur est butte à l'envie. Le mysticisme romantique voit dans le malheur le signe auguste, la marque d'élection mise par Dieu même au front de l'homme inspiré. La solitude et la souffrance ne sont pas la rançon du génie, elles en sont la source et la condition.

Thus the poet's sensibility is involved in the romantic idea of the poet as the man of fate. He has a greater emotional capacity than the herdman, and his response to society's rebuffs makes him a fated man. Society rejects the poet, who then suffers in solitude. He expresses his anguish either actively or passively; he turns against society or himself. In other words he is either a fatal or a fated man.

Consider Baudelaire's notion of the poet. He thinks that genius is a fatal gift which dooms the poet to pain, frustration, anguish, and that society is in open conspiracy against the poet. In "Bénédiction" he vividly describes how society persecutes the poet:[2]

> Dans le pain et le vin destinés à sa bouche
> Ils mêlent de la cendre avec d'impurs crachats;
> Avec hypocrisie ils jettent ce qu'il touche,
> Et s'accusent d'avoir mis leurs pieds dans ses pas.
>
> Sa femme va criant sur les places publiques:
> "Puisqu'il me trouve assez belle pour m'adorer,
> Je ferai le métier des idoles antiques,
> Et comme elles je veux me faire redorer;
>
> Et je me soûlerai de nard, d'encens, de myrrhe,
> De génuflexions, de viands et de vins,
> Pour savoir si je puis dans un coeur qui m'admire
> Usurper en riant les hommages divins!"

In another poem the albatross symbolizes the poet. For it is the great seabird which soars alone with ease into the heavens but lumbers about, encumbered by its wings when forced to earth, and then is tortured by sadistic sailors. Such is the poet's lot in a hostile society.

The figure of the doomed poet also recurs in Vigny. Chatterton as the fated man is foreordained to his tragic end by the structure of society. He cannot escape for even though he withdraws to the haven of the Bell home, he still feels the pressure of society. His romantic sensibility, which gives him the poet's sensitivity, also causes his suffering because it makes his suffering possible. Furthermore, the fated poet cannot, by withdrawing, abrogate the cause-effect relationship inherent in society. He must suffer because he is what he is. The fact that he is a poet draws the attention of man and the gods, arouses their disapproval, and starts a chain of cause and effect which inevitably destroys him. For once the poet attracts the notice of society, evasion is impossible and any resistance to destiny quite futile. The poet must walk the road of fatality to its natural end, once he has entered it.

Vigny is explicit in *Stello*. His mouthpiece, the Docteur-Noir, examines the languishing poet, Stello, and finds him mortally ill with poetic creativity—the gravest of human maladies. He warns that the disease, if not checked, will prove fatal. The poet is a sick man who has no place in modern society because it will not tolerate him. Yet the poet cannot change himself; he remains what he is and suffers for it. Again it is his peculiar sensibility which makes the hero a poet while simultaneously providing him a hypersensitive capacity for suffering. And he suffers because society rejects him.

Nerval's orphic hero suffers in a different way. The poet divorces his intellectual and social functions in his effort to evade society; he hopes to be free as a poet by canceling all social obligations. Yet this is manifestly impossible. As in *Aurélia* the poet may withdraw but he still continues to struggle with an introjected society. He cannot escape the social context. He is therefore fated in his struggle with society, even though he may no longer be in touch with it.

Nerval's hero battles an elusive social fantasm rather than an actual society. Since this struggle takes place in the poet's mind, Nerval's portrait of the hero is more psychological than Vigny's or even Baudelaire's. The pathology of Nerval's orphic poet is also more evident; he is in fact a schizophrenic hero. The hero is split by the separation of poet from his audience, society. Moreover, this split sets the scene for his struggle as the fated man. He differs from other heroes, as the fated man, since his struggle is internal rather than external—in his mind rather than in society. The stakes are also higher, and Nerval's poet does not bear the frightful stress of social rejection. He goes insane.

There are other men of fate who are victimized by their hypersensibility. For since the hypersensitive hero possesses a romantic sensibility unlike the herdman, his patterns of emotional response are exaggerated. This fact becomes clear as the man of fate squirms in the social context. In this setting his failure to respond normally causes him as a fatal man to destroy others wittingly or unwillingly, or he is destroyed as a fated man by his own hypersensibility. He expresses his energy either actively or passively, he is either the butcher or victim, and he may in fact be both at once. Still he remains the man of fate whatever role he plays, for he always acts according to a romantic notion of necessity in the social context.

Adolphe as a man of fate suffers from his hypersensibility as he struggles against society. He maintains a liaison in a culture which expects him to fill certain obligations. In this context fatality is the relentless march of events in which he and Ellénore are caught, against which they fight, to which they finally succumb. Adolphe studies himself in anguish against this background of ultimate defeat. He is aware, for instance, of the battle which his beloved, Ellénore, must fight first as another man's mistress and then as his own after she abandons her children. He discusses fatality in the following passage:[3]

Ellénore, en un mot, était en lutte constante avec sa destinée. Elle protestait, pour ainsi dire, par chacune de ses actions et de ses paroles, contre la classe dans laquelle elle se trouvait rangée; et comme elle sentait que la réalité était plus forte qu'elle, et que ses efforts ne changeraient rien à sa situation; elle était fort malheureuse.

Here fatality is equated with inevitability. Ellénore is powerless to extricate herself from this painful situation. Her
struggle is abortive and she is held increasingly fast in a web
of her own weaving. The entire novel is the record of the
destructive power of fate over Adolphe and Ellénore.

The novel also shows more. Adolphe and Ellénore are
fated as well as fatal. They exercise a destructive influence
on each other though this fact is perhaps truer of Adolphe
than Ellénore. He acts selfishly when he first seduces her. He
does not love her but simply wants to have a mistress like
his young aristocratic friends. Until he begins to court her,
Ellénore is for her part happily attached to her lover, whom
she has borne two children during ten years. Their relationship is almost that of marriage, but Adolphe is vain, impetu-
ous, importunate. No sooner does he seduce her, however,
than he tires of her and wants to rid himself of her. The rest
of the novel records the seesaw of his changing desire to
retain her, to get rid of her. In turn Ellénore clings to him
in a way that prevents him from entering a career; consequently her love is destructive. In short, their actions in their
tumultuous liaison hasten the foreordained, fatal end. While
she heeds her heart rather than her reason, Ellénore knows
from the beginning that their love is ill-starred. It is so dic-
tated by their social context.

Fatality as relentless progression is further evident in Constant's *Cécile,* a novel which greatly resembles *Adolphe* in
plot-structure, theme, and mood. The narrator says of his
beloved, Cécile:[4]

Je ne voyais donc pour elle que la ressource, triste il est vrai,
mais unique, de se résigner à la destinée qu'elle s'était faite, et je
m'étais promis que, de ma part du moins, rien ne serait tenté
qui pût troubler de nouveau cette destinée.

It is again evident that destiny is irresistible and that one
hastens his end, like Cécile, by the wrong behavior. Moreover, it is the fatal man who evidences this sort of behavior
since it is he who accelerates the progression of events toward
an inevitable end. In *Cécile* both the narrator and heroine

are caught in a cause-effect relationship like mice treading a wheel. Their efforts to escape only make the wheel turn faster. Fatality is once more necessity, and it causes a tragic pattern to evolve from a situation which possesses certain given ingredients. The key factor is the hero's conflict with society.

Dumas *père's Antony* testifies to the power of necessity. In this play Antony cannot enjoy Adèle's love because he is a bastard in a society which esteems birth and station rather than accomplishment and worth. He exclaims bitterly:[5]

. . . Le hasard, avant ma naissance, avant que je pusse rien pour ou contre moi, avait détruit la possibilité que cela fût; et, depuis le jour où je me suis connu, tout ce qui eût été pour un autre . . . réalité n'a été pour moi que rêve et déception.

Antony's disaster proceeds inevitably from his illegitimate birth, which precludes the possibility of station and hence of love, happiness, and honor in society.

Dumas observes that destiny is whimsical. Certain chance incidents intensify the progression of events which overwhelm the man of fate. Thus Antony explains the series of incidents which lead to his meeting Adèle:[6]

C'est que le hasard semble, jusqu'à présent, avoir seul régi ma destinée. . . . Si vous saviez combien les événements les plus importants de ma vie ont eu des causes futiles! Un jeune homme, que je n'ai pas revu deux fois depuis, peut-être, me conduisit chez votre père. . . . J'y allai, je ne sais pourquoi, comme on va partout. Si vous ne la nommez pas hasard, comment donc appelerez-vous cette suite d'infiniment petits événements qui, réunis, composent une vie de douleur et de joie, et qui, isolés, ne valent ni une larme ni un sourire?

Dumas's concept of chance is couched in social terms. Chance is mere fortuitousness, not the whim of the gods. But it can hasten the man of fate's destruction though it is clear that within the given context Antony's fate would ultimately be the same. Chance as a motor force speeds the progression to an inevitable catastrophe:[7]

. . . Une futilité me décide, un caprice me conduit, et, pourvu que je change de lieu, que je voie de nouveaux visages, que la rapidité de ma bourse me débarrasse de la fatigue d'aimer ou de haïr, qu'aucun lien ne se brise quand je pars, il est probable que j'arriverai comme les autres . . . au terme d'un voyage dont j'ignore le but, sans avoir déterminé si la vie est une plaisanterie bouffonne ou une création sublime.

Although the man of fate cannot modify the course of destiny or abrogate the power of chance, his hypersensitive response readily hastens his end. This is what Antony does as a man of fate.

His destiny is linked to his love for Adèle. Now since society forbids this love, he reacts in such a way that in time he becomes an agent of necessity. As a fatal man he speeds matters to a conclusion. As he explains, he no longer rebels against fate:[8]

Un seul lien m'attachait à ce monde; il se brise. . . . Et moi aussi, je veux mourir! . . . mais avec toi; je veux que les derniers battements de nos cœurs se répondent, que nos derniers soupirs se confondent. . . .

Antony executes his own fate because his hypersensibililty causes him to act in a way that contributes to his downfall.

René is another hypersensitive man of fate. There is a proportional relationship between his romantic sensibility and his attitude towards fate. His emotional involvement is correlated with his awareness of the role he plays, and a change in attitude towards fate entails a corresponding change in his romantic sensibility. In the following lines he equates fate with adverse fortuity:[9]

Tout m'échappoit à la fois, l'amitié, le monde, la retraite. J'avois essayé de tout, et tout m'avoit été fatal. Repoussé par la société, abandonné d'Amélie, quand la solitude vint à me manquer, que me restoit-il?

At this point he bemoans fatality without explaining the role of fortune; he is emotionally exhausted and disenchanted. He is passive. Nothing goes right for him, he cannot get along with others, he is a fated man. But as he later confronts the pain and disappointment, the frustration and hopelessness in his life, he feels different about fatality. The change is significant:[10]

Céluta pensa perdre la vie, en la donnant à une fille que l'on porta à son père, et qu'en versant des pleurs, il nomma Amélie. Cette seconde Amélie paroissoit au moment d'expirer: René se vit obligé de verser l'eau du baptême sur la tête de l'enfant en péril; l'enfant poussa un cri. Le baptême parmi les Sauvages étoit regardé comme un maléfice: Ondouré accusa le guerrier blanc d'avoir voulu faire mourir sa fille, par dégoût pour Céluta, et par amour d'une autre femme. Ainsi s'accomplissoit le sort de René; tout lui devenoit fatal, même la bonheur.

By drawing closer to others René becomes increasingly fatal, destructive, though unwillingly. For he becomes an active rather than a passive agent and he interprets fate in active terms:[11]

La fatalité qui s'attachoit à ses pas le repoussoit des deux hémisphères; il ne pouvoit aborder à un rivage qu'il n'y soulevât des tempêtes.

In his last letter to Céluta, his Indian wife, he states that fate, Providence, has pursued him ceaselessly.

Thus fatality acts upon him as an active hero in two ways. First, he acts passionately from his hypersensibility rather than temperately from his understanding. Second, his loved ones, like Céluta, misunderstand him because of his hypersensibility. He seems to be something he is not. It is a vicious circle. Fatality results from misunderstanding, and the cause-effect relationship continues to enmesh René. He makes an essential error in judgment, say, for which he suffers the inevitable consequence. Then the error entails more disaster through his hypersensitive reaction to the consequence. And the endless chain of cause and effect, of action and response, of deed and misinterpretation, continues to harm everyone. The following incident is typical:[12]

Depuis qu'il étoit père, sa tristesse étoit singulièrement augmentée. Il passoit des jours entiers au fond des forêts. Quand il revenoit chez lui, il prenoit sa fille sur ses genoux, la regardoit avec un mélange de tendresse et de désespoir, et tout à coup la remettoit dans son berceau comme si elle lui faisoit horreur. Céluta détournoit la tête, et cachoit ses larmes, attribuant le mouvement de René à un sentiment de haine pour elle.

Through such misunderstanding René repeatedly plays his role as the fatal man.

It is significant that in his final letter to Céluta he also discusses fate in terms of hypersensibility:[13]

. . . Il y a des existences si rudes qu'elles sembloient accuser la Providence et qu'elles corrigeroient de la manie d'être. Depuis le commencement de ma vie, je n'ai cessé de nourrir des chagrins; j'en portois le germe en moi comme l'arbre porte le germe de son fruit. Un poison inconnu se mêloit à tous mes sentiments: je me reprochois jusqu' à ces joies nées de la jeunesse et fugitives comme elle.

Now he conceives fate as a force actively seeking his destruction, whereas in the early part of the novel he regards fate as adverse fortuity. Moreover, that force is his hypersensibility. During the same time he ceases to be a passive hero and becomes an active hero; the direction of his romantic sensibility changes from inward to outward. He ceases to be entirely a fated man; his fatal aspect gains prominence. His self-condemnation is also explicit. René feels that he is victimized by *quelque principe de désordre,* his hypersensibility, which is closely related to fate. And he wonders whether ór not he may in fact impute his fatality to the gods. Chateaubriand resolves this question in his judgment of René:[14]

Il y a des familles que la destinée semble persécuter; n'accusons pas la Providence. La vie et la mort de René furent poursuivies par des feux illégitimes qui donnèrent le ciel à Amélie et l'enfer à Ondouré: René porta le double châtiment de ses passions coupables. On ne fait point sortir les autres de l'ordre, sans avoir en soi quelque principe de désordre; et celui qui, même involontairement, est la cause de quelque malheur ou de quelque crime, n'est jamais innocent aux yeux de Dieu.

By rejecting the notion that the gods pursue him Chauteau-briand underscores what René comes to realize. He himself is guilty. In spite of adverse fortuity he is guilty of having the emotional predisposition from which his difficulties spring as the fatal man and which seal his end. Clearly fatality is conceived in a social context, not a cosmic scheme. The gods are exonerated.

Hypersensibility is also interwoven with fatality in Hugo's *Hernani*. His role as a man of fate springs from his hypersensibility as expressed in the social context. Hernani analyzes himself:[15]

> Je suis une force qui va!
> Agent aveugle et sourd de mystères funèbres!
> Une âme de malheur faite avec des ténèbres!
> Où vais-je? je ne sais. Mais je me sens poussé
> D'un souffle impétueux, d'un destin insensé.
> Je descends, je descends, et jamais ne m'arrête.
> Si parfois, haletant, j'ose tourner la tête,
> Une voix me dit: Marche! et l'abîme est profond,
> Et de flamme ou de sang je le vois rouge au fond!
> Cependant, à l'entour de ma course farouche,
> Tout se brise, tout meurt. Malheur à qui me touche!
> Oh! fuis! détourne-toi de mon chemin fatal,
> Hélas! sans le vouloir, je te ferai du mal!

Hernani is blind action without thought—the incarnation of a romantic hypersensibility which veers out of control. He is fated by a consuming energy which he expresses blindly without respect to object. This is why he warns Doña Sol that he is liable to harm her; he says, in short, that just as he is fatal to others he might harm her in spite of himself. He is both fatal and fated because he cannot control his romantic sensibility.

While he seems aware that Hernani's hypersensibility accounts for his role as a man of fate, Hugo also explains his catastrophe in terms of the social structure. In other words, Hernani promises to give his life whenever Don Gomez demands it. As Hernani explains to Doña Sol: "Il a ma parole, et je dois la tenir."[16] It is inconceivable that a Spanish noble-

man of the period, at least in romantic fiction, should fail to
keep his promise—especially if it costs his life. Thus faithful
to his birth Hernani commits suicide. He is fated and destroyed by events acting upon him in and as a result of the
peculiar social structure of the age. His death—absurd to the
modern reader—is at least justified by the stringent social
code, though a cynic might doubt whether many Spanish
noblemen ever followed the code so literally. As an outlaw
Hernani harms others in his blundering way, and he is overwhelmed finally by the letter of the chivalric code. However
plausible this may seem, it is evident that he is best understood as a man of fate in terms of his hypersensibility and
the insuperable difficulties which it entails. A less sensitive
hero would manage to get into much less trouble.

Hugo's *Bug-Jargal* is another example of the hero's conflict
with society. The setting is in the slave insurrection in Haiti,
shortly after the French Revolution begins. Bug-Jargal, or
Pierrot, leads the Negro revolt although Habibrah, the dwarf,
is responsible for massacring the French colonists. Bug-Jargal,
the son of an African king, epitomizes nobility and justice.
The fatal situation arises in the following manner: Though
a slave Bug-Jargal is in love with Marie d'Auverney, who
comes to the islands in search of fortune. He returns her love
against a background of the Haitian holocaust. Bug-Jargal is
clearly a fated man who struggles against social injustice in
a context where he cannot conceivably win, for despite his
initial successes his ragtail army is helpless before the French
militia. Léopold is a fatal man inasmuch as despite his good
intentions he destroys Bug-Jargal, for chance arranges his
actions in a pattern that ultimately destroys the Negro. Consider in this connection the crucial episode in which Bug-
Jargal rescues Léopold at great risk to himself, despite his
love for Marie. But after a moment with Marie, Léopold
returns to his captor, Biassou, according to his promise:[17]

Dans trois heures le soleil sera couché. Ces paroles si simples me
glacèrent comme une apparition funèbre. Elles me rappelèrent
la promesse fatale que j'avais faite à Biassou. . . . Le brigand avait
ma parole, et il valait mieux encore mourir que de donner à ce

barbare le droit de mépriser la seule chose à laquelle il parût se fier encore, l'honneur d'un Français. . . . Je choisis ce que je devais choisir.

By returning to Biassou Léopold makes two fatal errors. First, he deserts Marie, whom the insurgents capture and kill. Second, he does not prevent Bug-Jargal from keeping his own fatal appointment with honor. For Bug-Jargal surrenders without explanation and is executed by Léopold's best friend, Thadée. Thus chance arranges the pattern of his actions in such a way that Léopold becomes fatal despite his good intentions and his exemplary character. His hypersensibility and exaggerated sense of honor account for the outcome. To this extent it is possible to say of Léopold d'Auverney, as indeed of any man of fate, that, given his temperament within a particular social context, the romantic hero necessarily acts as he does. In short, the man of fate is determined by these two essential factors, his temperament and the social context, which are in deadly conflict with each other. When his temperament is passive, he is a fated man; when active, a fatal man; but most often he is a combination. The result is in any case disastrous.

THE COSMIC CONTEXT

The romantic hero may also be a man of fate in a cosmic context, where a natural or supernatural force controls or directs the affairs of men. Now he may be an executor or victim of the gods or cosmic scheme, either a fatal or a fated man, or he may be both at once like the hero in the social context. But the essential difference is that the romantic writer conceives his hero as a man of fate in cosmic terms. Indeed the hero becomes a man of fate through conflict with a power in the cosmic context, though he is of course subsumed as a man within the social context.

Perhaps more than any other romantic writer Vigny is preoccupied with man in his conflict with the universe. His poems are mostly a succession of tableaux in which the man of fate is trapped by cosmic forces over which he has limited or no control. Fatality is the dominant motif which characterizes the human condition. Destiny is "une force inéluctable et pernicieuse, infligeant au Juste un châtiment immérité."[18] But while every man is involved in the human condition, only the romantic hero is sufficiently aware of his place in the cosmos to be much concerned with the problem of destiny. Moreover he derives his knowledge from his hypersensitive perception, his romantic sensibility.

Wisdom consists in man recognizing that cosmic forces hold all life in their grasp. Vigny records this conviction, among other places, in "Les Destinées":[19]

> Depuis le premier jour de la création,
> Les pieds lourds et puissants de chaque Destinée
> Pesaient sur chaque tête, sur toute action.

> Chaque front se courbait et traçait sa journée,
> Comme le front d'un boeuf creuse un sillon profond
> Sans dépasser la pierre où sa ligne est bornée.

> Ces froides déités liaient le joug de plomb
> Sur le crâne et les yeux des Hommes leurs esclaves,
> Tous errant, sans étoile, en un désert sans fond;

> Levant avec effort leurs pieds chargés d'entraves,
> Suivant le doigt d'airain dans le cercle fatal,
> Le doigt des Volontés inflexibles et graves.

Vigny testifies to his disillusionment and despair in a world where man cannot win any ultimate victories. The fated man is caught in a mechanistic universe which functions capriciously upon the affairs of men. For example, the course of the French Revolution, and thereby world history, changes during the scene of the Wheel of Fate in *Cinq-Mars* when a common soldier fails to wheel around his cannon on the Assemblée. Vigny implies that much of history is composed of such incidents, trivial in themselves, incalculable in effect. Those who suffer from such freakish whimsicality in the world-order are of course fated men, and their destiny is largely meaningless and tragic. This is the common lot. But whereas the herdman is ignorant of his role in the cosmos, the romantic hero does know and his knowledge entails deep spiritual anguish.

In "Les Destinées" Vigny discusses his notion of free will, which is the key problem in his analysis of the human condition:[20]

> Arbitre libre et fier des actes de sa vie,
> Si notre coeur s'entr'ouvre au parfum des vertus,
> S'il s'embrase à l'amour, s'il s'élève au génie,
>
> Que l'ombre des Destins, Seigneur, n'oppose plus
> A nos belles ardeurs une immuable entrave,
> A nos efforts sans fin des coups inattendus!
>
> O sujet d'épouvante à troubler le plus brave!
> Questions sans réponse où vos Saints se sont tus!
> O Mystère! ô tourment de l'âme forte et grave!
>
> Notre mot éternel est-il: C'ETAIT ECRIT?
> SUR LE LIVRE DE DIEU, dit l'Orient esclave;
> Et l'Occident répond : SUR LE LIVRE DU CHRIST.

Man is a mechanistic creature in a deterministic universe and has no free will. Such is Vigny's message. The God of Christian theology manipulates the affairs of men no less maliciously than the gods of antiquity, and the advent of Christianity has not really freed man. In both the Christian and the pagan worldview man is fated since he is manipulated without his knowledge and against his will. Man has no free will.

Vigny further treats the problem of free will in *Eloa*. In this poem Satan is both fatal and fated from the moment he exercises his free will. His egotistic rebellion against God disrupts the harmony which exists in nature. It becomes his mission to destroy rather than bear witness to God's creation, and he becomes the archetypal rebel. Ironically, however, Satan is not free after he rebels. For in his moment of choice and self-assertion he exchanges his former self, characterized by obedience and harmony, for a new self, characterized by defiance and discord. In short he is free to change his personality, but he is no longer free once he does so. He must afterwards act according to the new principle of his being, which, no less than the old, rigidly controls all his actions.

Eloa is an angel born of Christ's tear. She learns that the brightest and most beautiful of angels, Lucifer, has been cast from heaven. In his new dwelling-place he has neither friends nor loved ones; hell is his awful solitude. Her heart is moved and she goes to him out of pity. After seeing his anguish she sacrifices herself to be with him, to give love to a fellow creature. The plot-structure of Eloa is baldly simple. Yet the poem becomes subtle and complex as Satan acts in his role as the man of fate.

Vigny portrays Satan in the following verses:[21]

La mort est dans les mots que prononce sa bouche;
Il brûle ce qu'il voit, il flétrit ce qu'il touche;
Il ne peut plus sentir le mal ni les bienfaits;
Il est même sans joie aux malheurs qu'il a faits.

He is fatal, destructive, and his destructiveness emanates from a principle of discord. It follows that if Satan acts according to his nature his actions must be evil if his nature is evil. And the idea of necessity precludes free will. He is a fated as well as a fatal man.

Satan reveals the fatal aspect of his role when he boasts: "J'ai pris au Créateur sa faible créature."[22] The fated aspect of his role is implicit in the dénouement as he carries away Eloa:[23]

"Où me conduisez-vous, bel Ange?—Viens toujours.
—Que votre voix est triste, et quel sombre discours!
N'est-ce pas Eloa qui soulève ta chaîne?
J'ai cru t'avoir sauvé.—Non, c'est moi qui t'entraîne.
—Si nous sommes unis, peu m'importe en quel lieu!
Nomme-moi donc encore ou ta Soeur ou ton Dieu!
—J'enlève mon esclave et je tiens ma victime.
—Tu paraissais si bon! Oh! qu'ai-je fait?—Un crime.
—Seras-tu plus heureux du moins, es-tu content?
—Plus triste que jamais.—Qui donc es-tu?—Satan.

The contrast between his earlier defiance and this scene is striking. In the dénouement he lacks the activity, will, which he earlier voices. He takes no joy from his action and indeed has no freedom or will. He cannot act different because his actions are mechanistically determined. He is fated.

There are several implications to this fact. Every man is fated in Vigny's universe. Furthermore, it is difficult to define his notion of free will precisely. Is it, as he seems to imply, merely the rebellion against God and the cosmic order, and if so can man express free will only once—only in that rebellion? Afterwards he must act according to his nature, which is evil, and he is thus free, i.e., capable, only to do evil. Vigny does not resolve this enigma. What is important in this study, however, is not the resolution of this philosophical question, but rather the figure of Satan as a man of fate acting in his dual role in the cosmic context.

Vigny's poetry evidences several attitudes towards destiny. First, fatality as cosmic force is malignant but not necessarily capricious. Second, it is both malignant and capricious, and perhaps malignant because it is in fact capricious. Third, fatality results from the hero's conflict with the cosmic scheme.[24] There is moreover a fourth attitude, exemplified by Chatterton as a fated man, in which the hero struggles against society, with the catastrophe being rigorously determined without reference to cosmic fatality; this aspect of the hero has been previously mentioned. Now from the logical standpoint the first two attitudes are mutually exclusive, but Vigny is not overly concerned with the niceties of this distinction. He simply portrays man in a context where nature is the great operative power, and his distrust of nature stems from his belief that it is indifferent and cruel.

Thus his worldview is pessimistic, and his optimism represents man's conscious effort to alleviate, correct, or somehow direct the malignant forces of nature or the cosmos. In other words, even though man is fated and cannot win an ultimate battle and even though he must someday die, he can at least choose to die like a hero and have the satisfaction of having fought well against an unjust adversary. Such a theme seems pessimistic, but it is as optimistic as possible for a stoic like Vigny. For he would not consider a belief in unilinear progress as optimism but rather as a delusion.

The fated man fights cosmic indifference and cruelty by acquiring scientific knowledge. He controls the elemental force of nature to some extent through science, and he should resign himself to what he cannot control. The scientist is not omnipotent and progress is not unilinear. Yet as "La Bouteille à la mer" attests, the hero continues to engage nature and the cosmos.

Vigny presents a series of fated men in *Les Destinées*. He identifies nature as the immediate executioner in almost every poem. Throughout the different poems he is preoccupied with abstractions like nature, death, man, woman, God, which he symbolizes in the wolf, Samson, or Christ, and then shows his relationship to nature in his struggle against the cosmos. Thus the abstraction, man, stands up against the law of death and suffering in nature in the form of the dying wolf; and man's personal death becomes a triumph. Vigny agrees with Pascal that man is strong because, though infinitely fragile, he is yet a thinking reed and therefore superior to the blind forces which overwhelm him.

There is some uniformity in Vigny's ideas of the fated man.[25] The hero first discovers the laws of destiny and the human condition, then enjoys life while conscious of the evil inherent in nature and the structure of society. Hope never deludes the hero, who maintains stoic serenity by realizing that his weakness is the result of nature. He knows that, as a conscious agent, he is superior to the unconscious agent, nature, which destroys him. He must endure suffering and death as part of the universal law. Although he cannot win an absolute victory against nature, the hero may win contingent victories through advances in science. It is the duty of the poet, who knows that the hero is a fated man, to write of man's nobility as he is vanquished. In this sense defeat becomes victory.

Vigny is more concerned with the fated man than the fatal man. While it is true that the fatal man is destructive to others in a social context, he obviously cannot harm the gods, nature, or the cosmos. Thus the fatal man is a secondary motif while the fated man, who is victimized by all three, assumes prominence. Indeed the fatal man can be destructive only in the social context, even when his destructivity is motivated by his conflict with cosmic forces. This point will become clearer from Balzac's *Peau de chagrin*.

Raphaël Valentin, the hero, is both a fated and a fatal man. To understand the significance, however, one must know his story. He is a young scholar of a noble, destitute family. He falls in love with Countess Foedora, a Russian, and spends on her what little money he has. When he learns that she cares nothing for him, he starts to commit suicide. But by accident—or is it all part of cosmic design?—he wanders into an old curio shop, where the aged proprietor takes an uncommon interest in him. On learning that Valentin wants only to be with beauty before killing himself, the old man loses his temper and exclaims:[26]

Essayer! Si vous étiez sur la colonne de la place Vendôme, essaieriez-vous de vous jeter dans les airs? Peut-on arrêter le cours de la vie? L'homme a-t-il jamais pu scinder la mort?

Then he shows Valentin the wild ass's skin while expounding his philosophy of life:[27]

Avant d'entrer dans ce cabinet, vous aviez résolu de vous suicider; mais tout à coup un secret vous occupe et vous distrait de mourir. Enfant! Chacun de vos jours ne vous offrira-t-il pas une énigme plus intéressante que ne l'est celle-ci? Je vais vous révéler en peu de mots un grand mystère de la vie humaine. L'homme s'épuise par deux actes instinctivement accomplis qui tarissent les sources de son existence. Deux verbes expriment toutes les formes que prennent ces deux causes de mort: VOULOIR ET POUVOIR. Entre ces deux termes de l'action humaine, il est une autre formule dont s'emparent les sages, et je lui dois le bonheur et ma longévité. *Vouloir* nous brûle et *Pouvoir* nous détruit; mais SAVOIR laisse notre faible organisation dans un perpétuel état de calme. Ainsi le désir ou le vouloir est mort en moi, tué par la pensée; le mouvement ou le pouvoir s'est résolu par le jeu naturel de mes organes. En deux mots, j'ai placé ma vie, non dans le coeur qui se brise, non dans les sens qui s'émoussent; mais dans le cerveau qui ne s'use pas et qui survit à tout.

He explains the magical property of the skin. Its possessor

can satisfy all his wishes, but the skin shrinks with each grati-
fication. The owner dies when it reaches the vanishing point.
Valentin is delighted at the prospect of life becoming a joy-
ous means of suicide; death will come through his very satia-
tion with life. He joyfully accepts the wild ass's skin.

Eugène de Rastignac introduces Valentin to society again,
and this time Countess Foedora does not confuse him. He
satisfies his wishes, even his whims, but he soon is terrified to
find the ass's skin shrinking. Modern science is impotent as
all efforts fail to stretch it back. Valentin falls in love with
Pauline Gaudin, a young girl who loves him passionately,
but the skin shrinks whenever he embraces her. He escapes
to the Alps, where he kills a man and discovers that the skin
is disappearing almost before his eyes. In the meantime he
seems to be dying of consumption, but he knows his death
is really being caused by the wild ass's skin. He cannot reverse fatality. Eventually the skin vanishes, life runs out, and
Valentin dies from love in Pauline's arms.

It is evident that Valentin is a man of fate in both a social
and cosmic context. He reacts to a certain transpersonal force
in nature while he is in a social setting. To the extent that
he cannot escape this transpersonal force, he is of course a
fated man; to the extent that he harms others while trying
to escape, he is also a fatal man. For instance, he hurts his
friend, Emile, his faithful valet, Jonathan, and his beloved
Pauline, while struggling to reverse the movement of fate.
This transpires in the social context.

It is also clear that Balzac's notion of fate is one of cause
and effect. When Valentin wants something, the ass's skin
shrinks; when the skin shrinks, he tries to keep from wishing
further; but as the old proprietor points out, it is a man's
nature to wish, to want, to will. Thus Valentin is fated.
Fatality seizes him from the moment he accepts the ass's skin.
He is also fatal. His efforts to escape the power of fatality only
harm his friends and ultimately hasten the inevitable end.
Consequently, he is a clearer example of the fatal man acting
in the cosmic context than any of Vigny's heroes.

SUMMARY

Most previous commentators, including Praz, tend to consider only the most superficial aspects of the man of fate. Praz observes for example:[28]

Certain qualities can be noticed here which were destined to recur insistently in the Fatal Men of the Romantics: mysterious (but conjectured to be exalted) origin, traces of burnt-out passions, suspicion of a ghastly guilt, melancholy habits, pale face, unforgettable eyes.

It is, of course, undeniably true that many heroes evince such traits, particularly those from low romanticism *(le bas-romantisme)*. For instance, Barbey d'Aurevilly's *L'Ensorcelée* is filled with hexes, gipsies, curses, ghosts, crime, murder, suicide, illicit love; and a catalogue of such books might be compiled from the romantic period. Yet a study like Praz's tends to be descriptive rather than analytic, and it does not really afford an understanding of the man of fate, who is neither defined nor compared. Praz does not analyze individual men of fate or synthesize them in an understanding of the hero.

The romantic hero as a man of fate may be a fatal man, a fated man, or both at once. He acts in relationship to the cosmic or social context, and the matter may be tenuous and subtle. At all events, the romantic hero becomes a man of fate because he has two qualities which the herdman does not have. First, he is aware of his role, which is every man's role to a limited extent, in both society and the cosmos. Second, his hypersensitive response to this awareness, which involves his romantic sensibility, results in a conflict between self and society, between self and cosmos. Finally, chance may accelerate the movement of forces in play, but it cannot set into movement forces which do not already exist in the hero himself. The man of fate's catastrophe is due to the interplay of these conflicting forces.

THREE

HYPERSENSIBILITY
AND THE PATHOLOGICAL HERO

ROMANTIC writers do not esteem classic notions of the normal or the ideal man; indeed, the romantic hero tends to be the antithesis of classic balance and reason. Strong currents of pathology run through the romantic movement. It is of course difficult to define either normalcy or pathology, but it is nonetheless evident that romantic authors and their heroes are far from anyone's idea of normalcy and certainly far from their own. Consider Chateaubriand striking his pose, Gérard de Nerval dragging a lobster down the street, Baudelaire with his algolagnia, Barbey with his diabolical dandies, Hugo with his ouija boards; the list is limitless. It is certainly not by chance that the romantic hero sires the decadent hero.

Since the line separating sanity from madness is tenuous, it is difficult to ascertain when the romantic hero's sensibility becomes pathological. In this light it is best to say that the romantic hero is always a man of hypersensibility, and whenever his patterns of hypersensibility are exaggerated enough, he may be called a pathological hero. Some clarification is in order. Let it not be forgotten that in respect to "sensibility" the romantic hero shows a richer variety of response to emotional and sensory stimuli than the herdman; his hypersensibility is one of his distinguishing traits. Now the romantic hero may cultivate his hypersensibility from the hedonistic pursuit of pleasure or from the belief that heightened sensibility results in acuter perception; or he may be unaware that he is cultivating his hypersensibility. But two dangers are apparent, whatever his motives. First, he may be dulled by his hypersensibility; continuous excitement may at last terminate in a failure to respond emotionally. Second, hypersensitive responses may become exaggerated to the point of abnormality. The pathological hero develops at this point.

The pathological hero is still a self-conscious hero who possesses the two fundamental characteristics of awareness and romantic sensibility. He is acutely conscious of himself, his emotions, thought-processes, and often his own abnormalities; and as a man of hypersensibility he excites himself in an effort to key his senses up to greater level of perception. Such a romantic pursuit of knowledge is dangerous. It is, for instance, a medical truism that a man who is acutely aware of his respiratory system is likely to develop difficulties in breathing, for this body-process is meant to function without his *awareness*. Virtually all psychiatrists agree too that the unconscious, as part of the psyche, has functions which are best performed without becoming *conscious*. Then, knowledge derived by romantic self-consciousness can often be deadly. In his romantic pursuit of knowledge the hero moves through his hypersensibility into this dangerous area of acute awareness. Still it is only when he betrays greatly exaggerated forms of perception and response that he can be justifiably termed the pathological hero. Although the two types are closely related and although the latter grows in fact from the former, they are by no means identical. Every romantic hero is a man of hypersensibility, but despite this fact he is not necessarily pathological.

Egocentrism is one of the romantic hero's most salient traits, but it becomes pathological only if it passes into egomania. The hero is understandably egocentric. He rejects the basic similarities of man with men and emphasizes the points of difference, particularly between himself and the herdman. To a large extent he is justified in believing he is unique; he knows that his perceptions and sensations are not those of ordinary men. He attributes this difference to an inherent quality which he tends to call his genius and which is in actuality the romantic sensibility. Since he knows that the individual necessarily interprets the world in his own light, he logically infers that the superior man has better perception. Such is the basis for his egocentrism, and the danger of such a belief is apparent. He becomes too introspective, too preoccupied with self, and egocentrism moves easily into the pathology of egomania. Moreover, the romantic hero evinces without exception a greater or smaller degree of egocentrism, which of course provides fertile soil for the growth of the pathological hero.

Consider René in this connection. His egocentrism is often accentuated to the point of egomania. He is a solitary preoccupied with self, his own desires, emotions, sensations; and he is dissatisfied with the world because it is not equal to his prodigious appetite. Hence he travels in search of new sensations, prompted by a vague urge which is neither concretely expressed nor ever fructified. Other men tend to become shadowy, and he projects his feelings into nature—the pathetic fallacy. He is the center of his universe, the sun of all mankind.

Le Père Souël, a perceptive Indian, recognizes his difficulty. He judges René after hearing his story:[1]

Rien, dit-il au frère d'Amélie, rien ne mérite, dans cette histoire, la pitié, qu'on vous montre ici. Je vois un jeune homme entêté de chimères, à qui tout déplaît, et qui s'est soustrait aux charges de la société pour se livrer à d'inutiles rêveries. On n'est point, monsieur, un homme supérieur parce qu'on aperçoit le monde sous un jour odieux. On ne hait les hommes et la vie que faute de voir assez loin.

He says in essence that René's sin is pride. He argues that René unjustly demands recognition from his fellows because he feels superior. René feels isolated, unloved, when he does not receive this recognition; the proud hero is overwhelmed by his spleen and disgust. Since the world cannot satisfy him, he longs for a vague infinity and whets his jaded emotions by turning to the exotic. He turns to classical civilization and the New World in his egocentric quest, but he finds nothing of lasting satisfaction. Boredom inevitably follows his emotional revels, depression his moments of elation. In short, pride impels him as a wanderer on the romantic quest, but it also defeats him at the point when his egocentrism becomes egomania.

His egocentrism passes naturally into egomania. Because he is so painfully aware of the dichotomy reality-ideality, René often lapses into abulia, a state which paralyzes his will and keeps him from acting. He also turns to sensation because he disdains action, and Chactas explicitly warns him in this connection:[2]

O René, si tu crains les troubles du coeur, défie-toi de la solitude: les grandes passions sont solitaires, et les transporter au désert, c'est les rendre à leur empire.

He ignores Chactas' advice and continues to withdraw from society until he is finally victimized by his hypersensibility:[3]

Se renfermant au sein de ses douleurs et de ses rêveries, dans cette espèce de solitude morale, il devenoit de plus en plus farouche et sauvage: impatient de tout joug, importuné de tout devoir, les soins qu'on lui rendoit lui pesoient; on le fatiguoit en l'aimant. Etoit-il agité de remords ou de passions? cachoit-il des vices ou des vertus? c'est ce qu'on ne pouvoit dire.

This egomaniac withdrawal into himself portends destruction. He abandons the real world and then painfully realizes that cerebral satisfactions are no opiate.

Adolphe is another romantic egotist. "Je veux être aimé," he says in the beginning of the novel, "et je regardais autour de moi."[4] The background of this statement is revealing. One of his friends contracts a liaison with a married woman; and not to be outdone Adolphe thinks of Ellénore, whose relationship to her lover is sanctified by two children and ten

years of fidelity if not by marriage. He callously determines
to seduce her. Then this liaison results not from love but
rather from his egocentric quest of sensation. Adolphe wants
to be loved, he feels he must be loved, and he is willing to
destroy others in love. However, he can return only a waver-
ing affection, not love, because of his egocentrism. In other
words his selfishness, which prompts him to seduce Ellénore,
keeps him from loving her. And his egocentrism becomes
egomania when, for instance, abulia paralyzes his will or
when he takes pleasure in suffering or inflicting pain. His
algolagnia results from his egomania inasmuch as he makes
himself the center of his world; he suffers and inflicts pain
in reference to his hypersensibility.

Sénancour's Obermann egotistically absorbs the world into
himself. His ego is so diffuse that he can hardly distinguish
between himself and nature:[5]

Je n'aime, il est vrai, que la nature; mais c'est pour cela qu'en
m'aimant moi-même je ne m'aime point exclusivement, et que
les autres hommes sont encore, dans la nature, ce que j'en aime
davantage. Un sentiment impérieux m'attache à toutes les impressions aimantes; mon coeur, plein de lui-même, de l'humanité,
et de l'accord primitif des êtres n'a jamais connu de passions
personnelles ou irascibles. Je m'aime moi-même, mais c'est dans
la nature, c'est dans l'ordre qu'elle veut, c'est en société avec
l'homme qu'elle veut, c'est en société avec l'homme qu'elle fit,
et d'accord avec l'universalité des choses.

His love for nature is a flooding sentiment, and as an organ
of perception his ego no longer distinguishes self properly
from nature. Since he attempts to incorporate reality into
himself, his romantic mysticism may be considered a pathological involvement of the ego, the self. "Il faut avoir de
l'amour-propre,"[6] he repeatedly says, whereas the religious
mystic rejects egotism. In Obermann as in René and Adolphe
egocentrism passes into egomania.

Egotism motivates Stendhal's Julien Sorel, who personifies
ambition in *Le Rouge et le noir*. Throughout the novel he
tries to enhance his position by manipulating others; in the

end he is victimized by his ego when he oversteps himself. He becomes an egomaniac when his reason no longer sets a limit on possibililty. His reading reflects his basic character early in the book:[7]

> . . . *Les Confessions* de Rousseau. C'était le seul livre à l'aide duquel son imagination se figurait le monde. Le recueil des bulletins de la grande armée et le *Mémorial de Sainte-Hélène* complétaient son Coran. Il se serait fait tuer pour ces trois ouvrages. Jamais il ne crut en aucun autre.

He idolizes Rousseau and Napoleon, two of the greatest egotists of modern times. He admires them for their stark honesty as they reveal themselves as titans of egomania and the will to power. Yet Sorel learns to camouflage his own egotistic will, since he realizes that only deception brings success, and he becomes a hypocrite:[8]

> Tout à coup, Julien cessa de parler de Napoléon; il annonça le projet de se faire prêtre, et on le vit constamment, dans la scie de son père, occupé à apprendre par coeur une bible latine que le curé lui avait prêtée. Julien ne faisait paraître devant lui que des sentiments pieux. Qui eût pu deviner que cette figure de jeune fille, si pâle et si douce, cachait la résolution inébranlable de s'exposer à mille morts plutôt que de ne pas faire fortune?

His egocentrism becomes egomania almost imperceptibly in this moment of decision. For after discovering that only two roads are open to success—the red and the black, the army and the church—he hypocritically chooses the black without believing in anything other than his will to power. He says to Mme Rênal revealingly: "Je suis petit, Madame, mais je ne suis pas bas."[9] He embarks on his career of hypocrisy, "s'étant voué à ne jamais dire que des choses qui lui semblaient fausses à lui-même."[10] He is determined to improve his lot at all cost, and his egomaniac will to power leads naturally to subterfuge. For instance his liaison with Mme de Rênal "était encore de l'ambition; c'était de la joie de posséder, lui pauvre être si malheureux et si méprisé, une femme aussi belle."[11] He imagines himself as a kind of superman:[12]

Il craignait un remords affreux et un ridicule éternel, s'il s'écartait du modèle idéal qu'il se proposait de suivre. En un mot, ce qui faisait de Julien un être supérieur fut précisément ce qui l'empêcha de goûter le bonheur qui se plaçait sous ses pas.

Thus his egocentrism becomes egomania, which he increasingly expresses as a demonic will to power.

Egotism is also the dandy's basic trait. He has a rage to be different from other men:[13]

C'est la force de l'originalité anglaise, s'imprimant sur la vanité humaine,—*cette vanité ancrée jusqu'au coeur des marmitons,* et contre laquelle le mépris de Pascal n'était qu'une aveugle insolence,—qui produit . . . le Dandysme.

Dandyism is at once the assertion of self and the deliberate cultivation of hypersensibility:[14]

C'est une manière d'être, entièrement composée de nuances, comme il arrive toujours dans les sociétés très vieilles et très civilisées, où la comédie devient si rare et où la convenance triomphe à peine de l'ennui. . . . Elle résulte de cet état de lutte sans fin entre la convenance et l'ennui.

The dandy's pride leads him to protest against social uniformity by asserting himself. Perhaps he is in this respect an early example of the "outsider" in Modern Western culture. Canu formulates the dandy's credo:[15]

Notre mission essentielle est de sauver notre âme, ce reflet de Dieu, unique et irremplaçable entre tous ces autres, que chacun d'entre nous apporta en naissant.

The dandy differs from the herdman by having a self to assert, not a mere reflection of the herdsoul; and this difference is primarily rooted in his patterns of response and perception, i.e., his hypersensibility. In this way the dandy as an egotist tends to become an egomaniac.

Indeed such a romantic egomaniac is the dandy's concept of the ideal man. Consider in this respect the herdman, who is fragile and easily destroyed. The dandy is superior to the herdman by possessing an invincible weapon: While exerting a powerful, usually malignant, influence on others, the dandy refuses to be caught in the web of circumstance of the cause-effect relationship inherent in society. In theory he does not suffer for his actions because he egomaniacally refuses to be involved. This point is justified by examining the dandy more closely.

Dandyism is more than a cult or a literary pose. It is indeed a philosophy of life which has historical roots in society:[16]

Nulle part l'antagonisme des convenances et de l'ennui qu'elles engendrent ne s'est fait plus violemment sentir au fond des moeurs qu'en Angleterre, dans la société de la Bible et du droit, et peut-être est-ce de ce combat à outrance, éternel, comme le duel de la Mort et du Péché dans Milton, qu'est venue l'originalité profonde de cette société puritaine. . . .

Thus the essence of dandyism, "le culte de soi-même,"[17] lies in the conflict of the superior man, the dandy, with society. He refuses to be constrained by the temporal laws of society, and he refuses to submit to the indignities of emotional involvement. The weapon he uses for self-protection is his cold, haughty demeanor, his frigid detachment from society:[18]

Le dandysme de Barbey, c'est la ruse de guerre d'un Normand qui ne veut pas s'abandonner à l'impuissance ou à la défaite, qui s'arme d'indifférence, de froideur, d'élégance hautaine, d'impertinence distinguée, comme d'un bouclier d'abord, d'une bonne lame ensuite, pour esquiver les coups ennemis et y riposter. . . .

With such a formidable weapon he can destroy without fear of retaliation and manipulate others without fear of being used himself. For whatever they do to his body, his real self— his unique, inner being—remains unharmed because it remains untouched. The dandy feels he cannot be destroyed emotionally if he cannot be emotionally moved.

Thus the dandy reacts against the cause-effect relationship which applies to other men. He wishes no less than the stoic to free himself from the bonds of emotional attachment, but of course his means are fundamentally different. Unlike the stoic he asserts himself in his rage to be different and may destroy others, but he will not in turn be victimized by their self-assertion. The stories in Barbey's *Les Diaboliques* testify to his destructive power.[19] At least in theory the dandy is always active, never passive, as he explains in the following credo:[20]

Sembler maître de soi, ne trahir par sa mise comme par sa conduite, aucun attachement particulier, telle est la meilleure méthode pour dominer les autres, ou, au minimum, éviter leur emprise.

His frigid self-assertion serves admirably as protective armor.

Yet this represents the dandy in his theoretical form as an ideal. There is a philosophical basis for his egomania in theory, but while some dandies conform to this concept of the ideal man, the deviations are much commoner. Barbey's dandies illustrate the ideal, the cold egomaniac who refuses to participate in society; but Baudelaire's dandies are involved in and suffer from the pains of life. There is nonetheless some indication that even Baudelaire has the same concept of the ideal dandy, as "Don Juan aux enfers" illustrates. However, other Baudelairean dandies are emotionally bound to the men and women who destroy them. Their hypersensibility is expressed in relationship of dandy with object and not in that of dandy with self. In short, the literary manifestations do not always conform to the type or the theory underlying the type, but there is in theory an ideal dandy best understood in terms of egocentrism and egomania. As a man of hypersensibility he is a type of the romantic hero, and his egocentrism often becomes pathological in the form of egomania. In this case the dandy becomes a pathological hero.

The man of hypersensibility possesses heightened powers of thought and perception as well as of feeling. Although this does not mean he is a "thinker," it does mean that he is a kind of cerebral hero. His emotionalism does not detract from his propensity to muse, brood, think, but it makes an important difference. He consumes his emotional energy in elaborate and intricate self-analysis; he watches himself as if he were someone else. The man of hypersensibility often becomes the homo-duplex.

The homo-duplex, for example, uses his hypersensibility to watch, study, and criticize himself. He does not necessarily have a multiple personality like Dr. Jekyll and Mr. Hyde; for although there are French heroes like Gautier's *Chevalier double,* they are much commoner in the German *Doppelgänger* tradition. There is an essential difference. In French literature the homo-duplex is internally conceived and executed; the man of intellect, as one personality, watches the man of hypersensibility as if he were indeed another person. In German literature the *Doppelgänger,* like Peter Schlemihl, actually meets another person who is his alter ego or double. The French homo-duplex is for the most part hypercerebral.

The homo-duplex expresses his hypersensibility in acute self-analysis. For instance, Adolphe dissects himself:[21]

Tout en ne m'intéressant qu'à moi, je m'intéressais faiblement à moi-même. Je portais au fond de mon coeur un besoin de sensibilité dont je ne m'apercevais pas, mais qui, ne trouvant point à se satisfaire, me détachait successivement de tous les objets qui tour à tour attiraient ma curiosité.

He is deeply conscious of his dual role as actor and spectator, and as the latter he studies the former. His personality is splintered. He feels strangely divorced from himself as the cold, logical half watches the human, emotional half. He vacillates as first the intellect, then emotion, gains ascendancy, so that he seems to be two men acting alternately rather than one man acting consistently. He becomes so expert as a homo-duplex he even suspects what he represses, as the following incident shows:[22]

"Adolphe, me dit-elle, vous vous trompez sur vous-même; vous êtes généreux, vous vous dévouez à moi parce que je suis persécutée; vous croyez avoir de l'amour, et vous n'avez que de la pitié." Pourquoi prononça-t-elle ces mots funestes? Pourquoi me révélat-elle un secret que je voulais ignorer? Je m'efforçai de la rassurer, j'y parvins peut-être; mais la vérité avait traversé mon âme; le mouvement était détruit; j'étais déterminé dans mon sacrifice, mais je n'en étais pas plus heureux; et déjà il y avait en moi une pensée que de nouveau j'étais réduit à cacher.

He almost becomes a homo-polyplex at such times, for not only is his intellect split from emotion but the intellect itself is also splintered. Throughout the novel he studies himself incisively, like an analyst probing his analysand's motives. His hypercerebration, an aspect of egocentrism and hypersensibility, tends to annihilate all passion, and he coldly studies the woman he loves. He cannot accept himself as a man of sensibility. He alternately analyzes or rationalizes his emotions, and the sharp cleavage between mind and emotion is never mended. And the homo-duplex becomes a pathological hero when his behavior results further in abulia or a schizophrenic split.

Obermann is explicit about the two beings in his breast:[23]

Je m'interrogerai, je m'observerai, je sonderai ce coeur naturellement vrai et aimant, mais que tant de dégoûts peuvent avoir déjà rebuté. Je déterminerai ce que je suis, je veux dire ce que je dois être; et cet état une fois bien connu, je m'efforcerai de le conserver toute ma vie, convaincu que rien de ce qui m'est naturel n'est dangereux où condamnable, persuadé que l'on n'est jamais bien que quand on est selon sa nature, et décidé à ne jamais réprimer en moi que ce qui tendrait à altérer ma forme originelle.

He postulates the existence of two distinct personalities, the first a knower, the second still a stranger to himself. He implies that a persona masks the real self from the knower, who is not the real self but only the intellectual agent frantically seeking to remove the mask. This is indeed his function as an intellectual agent.

Yet the homo-duplex is not always warring with himself. He may play a comparatively minor role as with Julien Sorel. While awaiting his execution Sorel indulges in a fantasy of what he might have been—an officer, a legation secretary, even an ambassador. But a voice within him suddenly cries to his astonishment:[24]

—Pas précisément, Monsieur, guillotiné dans trois jours. Julien rit de bon coeur de cette saillie de son esprit. En vérité, l'homme a deux êtres en lui, pensa-t-il.

But Sorel is rarely conscious of himself as a homo-duplex, and the theme is minor since it represents his involuntary reaction to stress.

The reader is not always certain with such men where the hypersensitive hero ends and the pathological hero begins. It is instructive to contrast them with another homo-duplex, in whom the pathological element is clearly marked. Although there may be doubts about the preceding heroes being either egocentric or egomaniac, either hypersensitive or pathological, there is no doubt in this case.

Gérard de Nerval formulates his own idea of the homo-duplex in this tense description:[25]

Une idée terrible me vint: "L'homme est double," me dis-je. —"Je sens deux hommes en moi," a écrit un Père de l'Eglise. —Le concours de deux âmes a déposé ce germe mixte dans un corps que lui-même offre à la vue deux portions similaires reproduites dans tous les organes de sa structure. Il y a en tout homme un spectateur et un acteur, celui qui parle et celui qui répond. Les Orientaux ont vu là deux ennemis: le bon et le mauvais génie. "Suis-je le bon? suis-je le mauvais? me disais-je. En tout cas, *l'autre* m'est hostile. . . . Qui sait s'il n'y a pas telle circonstance ou tel âge où ces deux esprits se séparent? Attachés au même corps tous deux par une affinité matérielle, peut-être l'un est-il promis à la gloire et au bonheur, l'autre à l'anéantissement ou à la souffrance éternelle?"

There are certain differences between his hero and Adolphe and Obermann. First, Nerval's tone is more desperate. Obermann regards the homo-duplex as a more or less universal occurrence, and stark desperation never enters Adolphe's conflicts as it does Nerval's. For Nerval not only says that there are two souls in one breast, as Adolphe and Obermann would concur, but also, and more importantly, that these two are enemies fighting to the death. Second, the two aspects of the homo-duplex, actor and spectator, are not only antipodal but invariably hostile. The split in Nerval is much sharper. By distinguishing between the good and evil genius rather than simply between actor and spectator, he implies that both good and evil can act, and since they struggle to control the same soul, the hero's destruction is inevitable in this struggle to the death. Third, it is also evident that Nerval's cleavage, unlike Adolphe's, is not only between intellect and emotion but also a fragmentation of each of these functions. At this point the homo-duplex ceases to be a man whose hypercerebration results in certain intellectual and emotional peculiarities. The matter is indeed graver. Nerval's hero clearly has a schizophrenic split.

Thus the homo-duplex becomes a pathological hero through these exaggerated forms of hypersensibility. Nerval's schizophrenic split is, for instance, accompanied by a separation of self from society. He rejects the world and turns to the fantasies of his dreamlife. Jeanine Moulin observes:[26]

Après 1841, "le rêve qui s'épanche dans la vie" emporte le poète vers une crise de conscience de plus en plus profonde de luimême; alors, sa solitude parmi les êtres, parmi les astres et parmi les croyances, lui permet de mesurer le tragique qui s'attache à la condition humaine et la vanité de toute lutte en ce monde. L'auteur d'Aurélia progresse indéfiniment dans le désert de ses angoisses.

And Nerval pays for this schizophrenic isolation with insanity. The split ultimately destroys the pathological hero.

The line between hypersensibility and pathology, as pointed out, is indeed tenuous. It is difficult to assess the homoduplex in this respect; yet it is clear that Nerval is a pathological hero whereas despite his hypersensibility Adolphe is not. Perhaps the problem may be resolved in the following way. The term "pathological" is only a convenient tag; a pathological hero like Nerval does not always behave irrationally. Then the advisability of using the term depends upon how frequently and intensely the hero is irrational; if often and intensely enough, the term "pathological hero" is warranted. But since most if not all romantic heroes, who are certainly men of hypersensibility, have "pathological" moments, the classification is not always neat.

The homo-duplex exemplifies the point admirably. He becomes pathological when, for instance, abulia paralyzes his will and he cannot act. Now abulia is a common malady for a homo-duplex like Adolphe. The actor and the spectator are at cross-purposes, the latter observing and commenting ironically upon the former's weakness and often trying to silence him. But if the man of intellect in the homo-duplex is completely dominant, the emotional half feels no impetus for action. The spectator, in this case, regards action as humiliating, pointless, abortive; and by dominating the actor he at least momentarily controls the homo-duplex. The will struggles but it is paralyzed by the intellect; hence the hero cannot act. Vacillation results when the forces are evenly divided and first one then the other takes ascendancy. But when is such behavior pathological? Does vacillation fall within the range of hypersensibility whereas abulia is pathological? It seems so as a rule of thumb, yet the judgment is not exact.

Many men of hypersensibility are sometimes afflicted by vacillation and abulia. Adolphe diagnoses himself for example:[27]

J'avais rejeté dans le vague la nécessité d'agir; elle ne me poursuivait plus comme un spectre; je croyais avoir tout le temps de préparer Ellénore. Il n'y avait plus en moi d'impatience: il y avait, au contraire, un désir de retarder le moment funeste.

Here as elsewhere rationalization characterizes the cerebral hero, and abulia runs thematically through his faulty self-analysis. Adolphe also says, betraying his abulia: "Je trouvais qu'aucun but ne valait la peine d'aucun effort."[28] Nor is he alone, for Obermann writes in a similar vein:[29]

L'ennui m'accable, le dégoût m'atterre. Je sais que ce mal est en moi. Que ne puis-je être content de manger et de dormir!

Chacun de mes jours est supportable, mais leur ensemble m'accable.

And René is "sans force et sans vertu."[30] In Musset's *La Confession d'un enfant du siècle* Octave laments after discovering Brigitte's perfidy with his best friend, Desgenais:[31]

Je sortis brisé, n'y voyant plus et pouvant à peine me soutenir. Je ne voulais jamais la revoir; mais, au bout d'un quart d'heure, j'y retournai. Je ne sais quelle force désespérée m'y poussait. . . . Enfin, je l'abhorrais et je l'idôlatrais; je sentais que son amour était ma perte, mais que vivre sans elle était impossible.

Octave's actions are childish and abortive, not mature and meaningful. His instability comes to border on pathology in the following scene with his mistress, Brigitte Pierson:[32]

Au sortir de ces scènes affreuses où mon esprit s'épuisait en tortures et déchirait mon propre coeur, tour à tour accusant et raillant, mais toujours avide de souffrir et de revenir au passé; au sortir de là, un amour étrange, une exaltation poussée jusqu'à l'excès, me faisaient traiter ma maîtresse comme une idole, comme une divinité. Ces élans de coeur duraient des nuits entières, pendant lesquelles je ne cessais de parler, de pleurer, de me rouler aux pieds de Brigitte, de m'enivrer, d'un amour sans bornes, énervant, insensé. Puis le matin venait, le jour paraissait; je tombais sans force, je m'endormais, et je me réveillais le sourire sur les lèvres, me moquant de tout et ne croyant à rien.

Such behavior is typical. After days of inertia or vacillation Octave finally lashes out with infantile fury. But once his spasm passes, he is again victimized by abulia as hypercerebration paralyzes his will. Like Adolphe and Obermann, Octave is a homo-duplex who scrutinizes his own actions as if he were another man. He ironically comments upon his own pathology. But unlike Nerval he does not remain pathological; he rather moves from hypersensibility to pathology and back again. Octave is, so to speak, a sometime pathological hero.

In abulia the hero blows an emotional circuit and is powerless to act; his abulia keeps him from responding adequately to society. This condition results in spiritual isolation which provokes the greatest anxiety and despair. For example, Obermann despondently writes his friend:[33]

J'ai des moments où je désespérerais de contenir l'inquiétude qui m'agite. Tout m'entraîne alors et m'enlève avec une force immodérée: de cette hauteur, je retombe avec épouvante, et je me perds dans l'abîme qu'elle a creusé. Si j'étais absolument seul, ces moments-là seraient intolérables; mais j'écris, et il semble que le soin de vous exprimer ce que j'éprouve soit une distraction qui en adoucisse le sentiment. A qui m'ouvrirais-je ainsi? quel autre supporterait le fatigant bavardage d'une manie sombre, d'une sensibilité si vaine?

But in fact he remains alone, "condamné à toujours attendre la vie";[34] and as he elsewhere recognizes, he is fundamentally unable to participate in society. For his hypersensibility disorganizes him to the point of pathology, and it prevents him from communicating with the world of which he feels a mystical but rarely an organic part. Such isolation is pathological, but it is not frequent or intense enough to justify calling Obermann a pathological hero. In an acuter form, however, it certainly accounts for Nerval's disintegration and final madness.

Even when the romantic hero's sanity is not at stake, the price of withdrawal from society is high and the hero suffers from his self-immolation. But this is not to say that his response is necessarily pathological. Vigny is a case in point. His disgust with the world, as Faguet says, is one current in the romantic worldview:[35]

Le monde est faux, la nature est insensible et cruelle. Il faut se réfugier dans la solitude, dans la contemplation sans espoir, et dans la pitié.

Perhaps only a hypersensitive man regards nature in this way, but the concept is by no means pathological. The withdrawal is stoic because Vigny knows that entanglement in life results in pain and frustration. Yet the withdrawal is sometimes so desperate that he almost breaks:[36]

Quittons le monde et allons à la nature, non comme à une

consolation, mais comme à un spectacle. Habitons la *maison roulante du berger;* transportons-la au gré du rêve et du désir; suivons le soleil avec elle d'horizon en horizon, ne laissons point de trace où nous ne voulons point laisser de souvenir; allons de spectacle en spectacle, en admirant, en oubliant, et en plaignant les hommes qui passent.

In other words, man puts out his feelers at his own risk since they may be, and usually are, trampled upon and broken. But if he chooses to be a spectator rather than an actor, he does not run the risk of painful involvement with society and life. Yet his solitude is a place of punishment at the same time that it is a refuge. While the hero is indeed safe from the pain of life, he also castigates himself by a painful withdrawal. He foregoes the possibility of pleasure as well as pain, and to the extent that he ceases to participate in society, he ceases to be human for even Vigny admits that it is human to participate. Then he evidences a pathological fear of and preoccupation with suffering which extends far beyond the stoic worldview; his romantic hypersensibility is involved. And while his hypersensibility forbids participation in life, it cannot prevent his suffering. In short Vigny cannot win; he places a double-bind upon himself. For he suffers no matter what he does; he makes it impossible for himself to win.

The preceding pages show how hypersensibility often and imperceptibly becomes pathology, just as egocentrism develops into egomania. Romantic heroes evince, of course, other pathological traits. Algolagnia, for example, abounds in romantic literature, and synesthesia is often a symptom though not in itself a pathological manifestation. Mario Praz treats romantic aberrations at length in *The Romantic Agony,* but it is nonetheless useful to exemplify by one writer, Baudelaire, how some of these traits are related to pathology and the highly developed romantic sensibility.

In some ways Baudelaire moves from the man of hypersensibility into the pathological hero. In "Les Correspondances" he formulates an idea of concomitant sensations, synesthesia, in which one sensation evokes another sense-impression, and there tends to be a general breakdown in the power the intellect exerts over sense-impressions. However, this state of affairs is due to the poet's hypersensitivity, not to pathology itself. At the same time it is only a step from pathology. When the senses become virtually autonomous, man surrenders the organizing power of his mind, and the sense-impressions themselves clamor for individual attention and they are not subject to the intellect's control. In short, the senses do not support reason as a *raison d'être;* they rather tend to enjoy impressions as goals in themselves. Such a breakdown in sensibility is unhealthy, and when it is sufficiently exaggerated, it is even pathological. Yet it is difficult, for example, to ascertain when Baudelaire's olfactory sense, coupled with his imagination, ceases to be merely hypersensitive and becomes truly pathological. But the fact that there is such a general breakdown indicates a pathological direction in which the hero is definitely moving.

There are other motifs. The theme of the homo-duplex is coupled with algolagnia in "L'Héautontimorouménos":[37]

> Je suis la plaie et le couteau!
> Je suis le soufflet et la joue!
> Je suis les membres et la roue!
> Et la victime et le bourreau!

The hero studies himself as he delights in experiencing and inflicting pain. Baudelaire further expresses his sadism in "A Celle qui est trop gaie":[38]

> Ainsi, je voudrais, une nuit,
> Quand l'heure des voluptés sonne,
> Vers les trésors de ta personne,
> Comme un lâche, ramper sans bruit,
>
> Pour châtier ta chair joyeuse,
> Pour meurtrir ton sein pardonné,
> Et faire à ton flanc étonné
> Une blessure large et creuse,
>
> Et, vertigineuse douceur!
> A travers ces lèvres nouvelles,

> Plus éclatantes et plus belles,
> T'infuser mon venin, ma soeur.

Sadism and masochism are recurrent aspects of his cult of evil, and it is apparent that the Baudelairean man of hypersensibility moves deliberately into the cult of perversity, whereas Octave, an earlier type, exclaims in horror:[39]

> Faire le mal! tel était donc le rôle que la Providence m'avait imposé! Moi, faire le mal! moi à qui ma conscience, au milieu de mes fureurs mêmes, disait pourtant que j'étais bon! Moi qu'une destinée impitoyable entraînait sans cesse plus avant dans un abîme et à qui en même temps une horreur secrète montrait sans cesse la profondeur de cet abîme où je tombais!

The difference in attitude is striking. Both heroes are cruel, both do evil, but the Baudelairean hero enjoys his cruelty, and he is deliberately and consciously perverse. There is of course a connection between Baudelaire's hypersensibility and his cult of evil. He is ravaged by hypersensibility, he feels a surfeit of emotion, and he can whet his jaded emotions only by abnormal sensations. The normal no longer suffices since such emotional response is deadened. The man of hypersensibility becomes the pathological hero.

In "L'Ennemi" Baudelaire describes the ravages of hypersensibility. He contrasts his stormy youth with his later years:[40]

> Ma jeunesse ne fut qu'un ténébreux orage,
> Traversé çà et là par de brillants soleils;
> Le tonnerre et la pluie ont fait un tel ravage
> Qu'il reste en mon jardin bien peu de fruits vermeils.
>
> Voilà que j'ai touché à l'automne des idées,
> Et qu'il faut employer la pelle et les râteaux
> Pour rassembler à neuf les terres inondées,
> Où l'eau creuse des trous grands comme des tombeaux.
>
> Et qui sait si les fleurs nouvelles que je rêve
> Trouveront dans ce sol lavé comme une grève
> Le mystique aliment qui ferait leur vigueur?

—O douleur! ô douleur! Le Temps mange la vie,
Et l'obscur Ennemi qui nous ronge le coeur
Du sang que nous perdons croît et se fortifie!

He says he has lived so intensely that it is difficult to rekindle the flames of normal sensibility. In short, his excesses have immunized him against further emotional experience. As Baudelaire testifies, the danger of hypersensibility is that it dulls the hero's emotional capacity, and this theme runs throughout *Les Fleurs du mal*. Hence he has to turn to the emotional possibilities of the cult of evil.

Abulia, despair, and ennui result from his emotional poverty. In "Le Mauvais moine" Baudelaire further depicts himself, this time as a victim of abulia:[41]

—Mon âme est un tombeau que, mauvais cénobite,
Depuis l'éternité je parcours et j'habite;
Rien n'embellit les murs de ce cloître odieux.

O moine fainéant! quand saurai-je donc faire
Du spectacle vivant de ma triste misère
Le travail de mes mains et l'amour de mes yeux?

In "La Cloche fêlée," "Recueillement," and the four "Spleen" poems, Baudelaire reveals his deep spiritual anguish. In "Réversibilité" he writes:[42]

Ange plein de gaieté, connaissez-vous l'angoisse,
La honte, les remords, les sanglots, les ennuis,
Et les vagues terreurs de ces affreuses nuits
Qui compriment le coeur comme un papier qu'on froisse?
Ange plein de gaieté, connaissez-vous l'angoisse?

His anguish becomes self-loathing in "Voyage à Cythère":[43]

Dans ton île, ô Vénus! je n'ai trouvé debout
Qu'un gibet symbolique où pendait mon image. . . .
—Ah, Seigneur! donnez-moi la force et le courage
De contempler mon coeur et mon corps sans dégoût!

Nearly every poem in *Les Fleurs du mal* illustrates a different psychological motif. Baudelaire's hypersensitive olfactory sense, for example, borders on an aberration. The pathologi-

cal hero is depicted in many ways: the condemned man dis-
interestedly smoking as he awaits his execution; violent and
sadistic lesbianism; nightmarish coition; vampirism. Each
motif is correlated with Baudelaire's hypersensibility, and an
emotion has been defined as pathological when it is sufficiently intense and exaggerated. Certainly in Baudelaire the
man of hypersensibility, the romantic hero, becomes the
pathological hero.

SUMMARY

The pathological hero has been discursively discussed because it is impossible to separate the categories of the man of
hypersensibility and the pathological hero. A man of hypersensibility is often "pathological" without warranting the
term "pathological hero" as a general judgment. The pathological hero grows from the man of hypersensibility.

One fact is clear. The romantic sensibility is the touchstone in understanding the pathological hero, for it provides
the fertile soil from which pathology can grow. Now the
romantic sensibility is simply one of the inherent qualities
which make the romantic hero what he is, and his sensibility
is actually hypersensibility or hypersensitivity in comparison
with the herdman's. He possesses this hypersensibility by
virtue of being a hero. This is to say that his emotional range
is greater than the herdman's, his perceptions acuter, his
responses more exaggerated.

The romantic hero may wish to cultivate his hypersensibility from a hedonistic pursuit of pleasure or from the conviction that hypersensitivity results in acuter perception. The
danger is apparent. It may become so intense and exaggerated
that it is in fact pathological. Yet the point of departure is
not always easy to define. When does Baudelaire's olfactory
sense cease to be hypersensitive and become pathological?
When does the homo-duplex cease to be a man who acutely
probes himself, and rather become a schizophrenic with a
cleavage between intellect and emotion and with a resultant
splintering of the personality? It is of course a question of
mental disorganization. But what does "normalcy" mean

when applied to the hero, the extraordinary man? A man like Octave sometimes behaves "pathologically" without justifying the term "pathological." The term "pathological hero" is warranted only when his irrationality is consistently pronounced like Nerval's. And even in this case there is no simple resolution to the problem. There are no sharp boundary lines.

The pathological hero is a descendant of the archetypal self-conscious hero. He is aware that his romantic sensibility differentiates him from the herdman, and he knows that his hypersensitivity is pregnant with possibility. He knows sensations which are far beyond the herdman's emotional range; thus he has insights, understanding, visions which the herdman cannot achieve. It is doubtful whether any romantic hero ever engages in a quest of insanity; yet it is nonetheless true that many a quest results in irrationality. Hypersensibility is indeed a road to knowledge, both of the world and the self, but it is a long, narrow, winding road fraught with many dangers. The pathological hero bears mute, and often vocal, testimony to the manifold dangers of romantic hypersensibility.

FOUR

THE POET-PROPHET

THE TERM *poet-prophet* is used to refer either to the author or his literary protagonist. Romantic literature is so autobiographical that the romantic hero often seems little more than the author's shadow. Since they possess the same traits and share the same motives and aims, it is therefore profitable to study them together.

The poet-prophet, as both author and protagonist, is subsumed by the self-conscious hero. He feels that he is unique, thinks more deeply, knows more than the herdman. The poet-prophets are unanimous on this point, but otherwise they reveal a great diversity. For instance, the poet-prophet may be separated from society by his wisdom and hypersensitivity; he may seek refuge in an ivory tower, engage on the romantic quest, become a rebel, or despair of communicating with the herd. Yet he may also become a leader through his wisdom and hypersensibility; he may be a visionary or seer, a man of action, or both at once. The lines of descent from the self-conscious hero often cross. In spite of these variations in type, however, the poet-prophet falls into three main categories—solitary, leader, and visionary.

Romanticism witnesses a fundamental change in the poet's place in society; a different kind of public confronts him.

Although this change seems cataclysmic, it is actually the product of social evolution. The increasingly utilitarian atmosphere of the seventeenth and eighteenth centuries lays the groundwork for the change, as the bourgeoisie replaces the aristocrats in financial areas. The cultural level tends to rise because money affords more leisure. The provinces become a reading market as well as Paris, and the idea of the public as a literary consumer becomes important for the first time in French history.[1] The French Revolution effects great social changes upon the eighteenth-century masses, and a new generation is reared in the post-Revolutionary era. The masses, formed in the tumult of industrialization and social change, turn to prose rather than poetry for their reading tastes. The modern newspaper is born and has a marked impact, and with the romantic movement the poet begins to emerge from the middle classes. The new poet must earn a living from his writing in a society where the bourgeoisie determines success or failure, and he correctly believes that the masses have little sympathy for him and his work. In short, the poet feels he no longer has a place.

The new society contrasts sharply with the traditional hierarchical society, where the poet has a definite role to fill no less than the soldier, priest, or king. To be sure, it is not a principal role, but the point is that the hierarchy assigns him a place. Yet his role is progressively undermined from the seventeenth century, when rationalism begins to be a potent force:[2]

The notion of the early poet as "vates" was of course a commonplace of the Renaissance, but it is interesting to find the seventeenth century emphasizing the *scientific* in addition to the moral, theological or political meanings which were supposed to be wrapped up in the fables of antiquity.

In the age of reason science precludes "poetic truth" as vague, imaginative, unverifiable. Hasard summarizes the general attitude:[3]

La poésie, comme on la maltraitait! On ne la comprenait plus, on ne l'entendait plus; on ne sentait plus passer dans les coeurs un souffle divin. On la réduisait à n'être plus qu'un des modes de l'art oratoire, son ennemi. Au lieu de chercher le profond dans l'âme, par un effort contraire à sa vraie nature elle allait vers l'extérieur, voulant arguer, prouver, résoudre. L'imagination était considérée comme une faculté inférieure. . . . Les Muses n'étaient plus des déesses; elles n'étaient autre chose que les différents moyens dont la Raison s'était toujours servie pour l'insinuer dans l'esprit des hommes.

The change is striking. Whereas patrons subsidize poets during the Renaissance, the poets of the seventeenth and eighteenth centuries find an audience by becoming the agents of reason and by writing for the cultured aristocracy. There are of course some great patrons during the period, but the trend is nonetheless apparent. In the romantic upheaval another situation confronts the poets. Now there are no more great patrons, the masses determine success, and the poet has no place in this new social order.

His problem is to find and fill a role in the new society. The problem is acute because, unlike his counterpart in the age of reason or the enlightenment, the romantic poet rejects rationalism as the motor force of poetry. At the same time the cultured reading public is conditioned to think that poetry is indeed the handmaiden of science and philosophy. Then the romantic poet feels he has no established place not only because the structure of the new society is different but also because he has a different idea of the function of poetry. All these factors tend to isolate the poet and cause a breakdown in his communication with society. In turn the poet reflects his concern with his fictional counterpart, the poet-prophet as hero; and his insecurity and isolation are two principal sources of the *mal du siècle*. But although the romantic poet is discomfited, he is convinced he knows what poetry really entails. He is self-consciously aware of the place the *vates* once held but which he does not hold, and he knows a solution must be found if the poet is to remain an organic part of society. He resolves this problem in different ways as a solitary, a leader, and a visionary.

THE SOLITARY

In his social role the poet-prophet must evidence one of two possible responses. He either belongs or does not belong to society as a functioning member. Yet he may in either case make great contributions. The solitary, or isolated poet, may for example direct his people from afar, while regretting his separation from the herd. Vigny, in particular, believes that the poet-prophet leads his people even when he is not of them. Baudelaire feels the poet cannot really speak to the herd, and it may be that the idea of the poet as a man writing only for other poets arises at this time. These antipodal responses are variations of the two attitudes which the solitary may take.

Baudelaire cries out in pain and indignation at his role. He says that society looks upon the poet with disgust and loathing. In "Bénédiction" even his mother exclaims:[4]

> Lorsque, par un décret des puissances suprêmes,
> Le Poëte apparaît en ce monde ennuyé,
> Sa mère épouvantée et pleine de blasphèmes
> Crispe ses poings vers Dieu, qui la prend en pitié:
>
> —"Ah! que n'ai-je mis bas tout un noeud de vipères,
> Plutôt que de nourrir cette dérision!
> Maudite soit la nuit aux plaisirs éphémères
> Où mon ventre a conçu mon expiation."

The poet is an object of ridicule in "L'Albatros":[5]

> Le Poëte est semblable au prince des nuées
> Qui hante la tempête et se rit de l'archer;
> Exilé sur le sol au milieu des huées,
> Ses ailes de géant l'empêchent de marcher.

He has no choice. He turns from the mundane world, where he is prey to crass, misunderstanding, sadistic men, to the haven of poetic fancy; only there is he safe. Rejected, ridiculed, despised in every conceivable way, he escapes through poetry:[6]

> Envole-toi bien loin de ces miasmes morbides;
> Va te purifier dans l'air supérieur,
> Et bois, comme une pure et divine liqueur,
> Le feu clair qui remplit les espaces limpides.

In "Elévation" as elsewhere Baudelaire refuses to participate and turns his back upon mankind. Yet he continues to participate as a poet, and he adds his own experience to man's knowledge. Men may come voluntarily to the Baudelairean poet-prophet through his poem, but he himself withdraws and despairs of mass communication. He is much too cynical, much too wise.

The poet's divorce from society is different in Vigny. Although Baudelaire comes in time to accept his withdrawal as inevitable and even necessary, Vigny indignantly proclaims that society persecutes a valiant, useful leader in the poet-prophet. He argues that society should rectify its error:[7]

La cause? c'est le martyre perpétuel et la perpétuelle immolation du Poëte.—La cause? c'est le droit qu'il aurait de vivre.—La cause? c'est la mort qu'il est forcé de se donner.

Whereas Baudelaire accepts his divorce as final, Vigny believes an enlightened society should effect a reconciliation. Baudelaire would sneer at the thought of an enlightened herd.

Vigny implies in *Chatterton* that the state should be responsible for its poets. In this play the young English poet Chatterton is ignored, then persecuted, because he is a poet-prophet; he becomes a pariah. Chatterton is destroyed in his fatal conflict with society. He breaks down and finally commits suicide. Before his death, however, he characterizes himself in the following words:[8]

Je n'en sais rien, mais jamais je ne pus enchaîner dans des canaux étroits et réguliers les débordements tumultueux de mon esprit qui toujours inondait ses rives malgré moi. J'étais incapable de suivre les lentes opérations des calculs journaliers, j'y renoncerai le premier. J'avouai mon esprit vaincu par le chiffre, et j'eus besoin d'exploiter mon corps.

Although a genius, Chatterton is childishly helpless before society. Vigny argues that the poet-prophet is properly responsible only to himself for using his genius, while society should take charge of his personal welfare. And the isolated poet, the solitary, belongs and contributes to society in the only way he can, through his poetry. He should not be concerned with diurnal needs.

Vigny emphasizes that the poet-prophet is not just a writer. He carefully distinguishes between the poet, *le grand écrivain*, and *l'homme de lettres:*[9]

Mais il [le poète] est une autre sorte de nature, nature passionnée, plus pure et plus rare. Celui qui vient d'elle est inhabile à tout ce qui n'est pas l'oeuvre divine, et vient au monde à de rares intervalles, heureusement pour lui, malheureusement pour l'espèce humaine. Il y vient pour être à charge aux autres, quand il appartient complètement à cette race exquise et puissante qui fut celle des grands hommes inspirés.

Le grand écrivain and *l'homme de lettres* are literary prostitutes, for they write for fame and money rather than from the compulsion of their imagination like the true poet. Vigny observes that they are masters of themselves and write for the market, whereas the true poet is beside himself and writes his knowledge of the Word. He is in the tradition of the *vates*, the divine madman, the seer. Therefore the state should take charge of his daily affairs.

Poetic creativity is a disease. It afflicts Stello, for example, and the Docteur-Noir prescribes the following cure: If he is determined to be a poet against reason, Stello should at least separate his poetic and social functions. He should give Caesar his due, then accomplish his mission in solitude. He should always keep in mind the fate of Gilbert, Chatterton, Chénier, if he intends to pursue a calling which entails unhappiness; and he should remember that hope is man's last delusion. Such is the message of the Docteur-Noir, or reason, to Stello, or poetic genius. Vigny again warns that the poet's isolation is fatal because the poet is inevitably isolated from society.

The true poet pursues his calling despite rebuff and disaster because, ironically, he has a social mission to fill. He can elevate man. He is the wise man who discerns truth unfathomable by the herd. Vigny develops this theme in "La Bouteille à la mer," *Stello, VII, XVII,* and it recurs throughout *Le Journal d'un poète.*

Vigny's poet-prophet is a cross between the *magus,* wise man, and *vates,* seer. He is afflicted with divine madness, yet is the practical leader of his people—if they would only follow him. Though separated from society, he possesses the knowledge which society needs. Thus he participates from afar, sometimes leading the herd without its will, sometimes with its will but never its affection. Moïse is such a solitary:[10]

> Sitôt que votre souffle a rempli le berger,
> Les hommes se sont dit: "Il nous est étranger";
> Et leurs yeux se baissaient devant mes yeux de flamme,
> Car ils venaient, hélas! d'y voir plus que mon âme.
> J'ai vu l'amour s'éteindre et l'amitié tarir,
> Les vierges se voilaient et craignaient de mourir.
> M'enveloppant alors de la colonne noire,
> J'ai marché devant tous, triste et seul dans ma gloire,
> Et j'ai dit dans mon coeur: Que vouloir à présent?
> Pour dormir sur un sein mon front est trop pesant,
> Ma main laisse l'effroi sur la main qu'elle touche,
> L'orage est dans ma voix, l'éclair est sur ma bouche;
> Aussi, loin de m'aimer, voilà qu'ils tremblent tous,
> Et, quand j'ouvre les bras, on tombe à mes genoux.
> O Seigneur! j'ai vécu puissant et solitaire,
> Laissez-moi m'endormir du sommeil de la terre.

God elects a poet-prophet like Moïse to bring his Word to the herd. But while he participates in society by delivering God's message, he suffers from his agonizing isolation. And once his task is over, he is superseded by another poet-prophet, just as Josué leads the people when Moïse dies. He is a divine instrument, not a man.

The poet-prophet fills his social role differently in "La Bouteille à la mer." The hero is a scientist whose message is utilitarian:[11]

Le vrai Dieu, le Dieu fort est le Dieu des idées!
Sur nos fronts où le germe est jeté par le sort,
Répandons le savoir en fécondes ondées;
Puis, recueillant le fruit tel que de l'âme il sort,
Tout empreint du parfum des saintes solitudes,
Jetons l'oeuvre à la mer, la mer des multitudes:
—Dieu la prendra du doigt pour la conduire au port.

He is illumined by patient study rather than by divine revelation. But he still suffers from the isolation which, ironically, his social role imposes on him in his effort to "assurer un avenir meilleur aux destinées humaines."[12]

The poet-prophet is interested in beauty as well as in truth. Vigny explains his esthetic function:[13]

Il y a, dans les oeuvres d'art, deux points de vue: l'un philosophique, l'autre poëtique. Le point de vue philosophique doit soutenir l'oeuvre, drame ou livre, d'un pôle à l'autre, précisément comme l'axe d'un globe; mais le globe, dans sa forme arrondie et complète, avec ses couleurs variées et brillantes, est une image de l'art qui doit être toujours en vue, en tournant autour de son atmosphère. . . . Réchauffer plutôt qu'enseigner.

In short, he argues that the poet-prophet is an artist as well as a *magus* and *vates,* and that these two aspects are complementary rather than mutually exclusive. It is nevertheless possible to realize one aspect without succeeding in the other. For example, the scientist perceives truth, but he is obviously not an artist, just as Gautier, say, is concerned with art without propounding a real theory of beauty. Ideally, however, the poet-prophet succeeds in both aspects of his dual role. If his social message is unheeded, he can enjoy the message—a thing of beauty in itself—as a work of art. The poem affords compensation even when the meaning, i.e., the Word, is misunderstood and ignored. In this case the poet-prophet may retire to his ivory tower and find quietistic release in contemplating art as beauty rather than by considering it as a social message. Here is an initial form of the theory of *l'art pour l'art.*

When he transmits a message to the herd, he is concerned with two problems—one specific, the other general. The specific problem is to deliver the Word, i.e., message, so that the herd may effect any needed reforms. The general problem involves the poet-prophet's concern with the delivery of the Word. What is the Word, i.e., poetic message? What indeed is poetic communication?

Vigny does not clearly distinguish between the different modes of poetic perception—*knowing* and *knowing about*. But he does intimate that the imagination effects the poetic communication, i.e., the Word:[14]

La seule faculté que j'estime en moi est mon besoin éternal d'organisation. A peine une idée m'est venue, je lui donne dans la même minute sa forme et sa composition, son *organisation complète.*

He touches upon the imagination in his passages on genius,[15] the poetic soul,[16] the contemplative soul,[17] poetic fancy,[18] inspiration,[19] the function of the symbol,[20] and most explicitly in "La Flûte"[21] without ever formulating a clear concept. He does not analyze poetic knowledge; he merely states that the poet-prophet delivers his message, the Word, to the people, just as Moïse descends the sacred mountain with God's commandments. As the most classical of romantics Vigny is discursively analytical; he retains the classic distinction between pleasing and instructing as the twin aims of art, and he does not formulate a concept of suprarational understanding by means of the poetic experience. He believes that the poet-prophet as a solitary must somehow communicate with the herd, but he does not resolve the fundamental problem of poetic communication itself.

THE LEADER

Hugo states baldly that "le poète est prêtre."[22] The poet acts as the prophet or priest of the god Reality, which he apprehends through a mystical experience. Discursive reason, which is characteristic of classic understanding, is foreign to Hugo. He simply sees and knows. He derives his knowledge of reality immediately and suprarationally. Furthermore he is not a solitary.

Hugo resolves the poet's isolation differently from Bau-

delaire and Vigny. He believes that the poet-prophet is invariably linked to his people and that he leads them to
enlightenment, redemption, social progress.[23] Thus good
poetry is a utilitarian form of communication; it has a definite social purpose. Hugo elaborates this position in his
poetry and throughout his many prefaces.

He repeatedly symbolizes the poet-prophet as the magus:[24]

Nous venons de prononcer ce mot: mage. Ce poëte en effet, par
moments, comme, Job, officie. On dirait qu'il exerce sur la nature,
sur les peuples, et jusque sur les dieux, une sorte de magisme.
Il reproche aux bêtes leur voracité. Un vautour qui saisit, malgré
sa course, une hase pleine, et qui s'en repaît, "mange toute une
race arrêtée en sa fuite."

It is his sacred function to transmit the Word to the people.
However, they do not always accept his message unquestion-
ingly or follow it willingly. The magus frequently suffers
while delivering the Word:[25]

Le voyant chargé d'éclairer la nuit humaine, parce qu'il pénètre
ainsi, divin, parmi les êtres adonnés au mal, ne peut que
provoquer leur colère, et souffrir. Plus sa mission est vaste, plus
il souffre. . . .

Yet it is his duty to immolate himself as a Messiah to save his
people, irrespective of their worth or gratitude.[26] His mission
is explicit:[27]

C'est surtout à réparer le mal fait par les sophistes que doit
s'attacher aujourd'hui le poëte. Il doit marcher devant les peuples
comme une lumière et leur montrer le chemin. Il doit les ramener
à tous les grands principes d'ordre, de morale et d'honneur; et,
pour que sa puissance leur soit douce, il faut que toutes les fibres
du coeur humain vibrent sous ses doigts comme les cordes d'une
lyre. Il ne sera jamais l'écho d'aucune parole, si ce n'est de celle
de Dieu. Il se rappellera toujours ce que ses prédécesseurs ont
trop oublié, que lui aussi il a une religion et une patrie.

Then the poet-prophet is a wise man who has both sacerdotal
and social functions, and the word "philistines" or "bourgeois" might well replace "sophists" in this quotation.

Though linked with his people, the poet-prophet is also
an intermediary between God and man. He stands midway
between heaven and earth. He communicates with God
through divine inspiration, then reveals the Word to God's
people. His role is always to dominate nature by combatting
evil, to interpret the universal symbolism in nature, to serve
as mediator between matter and the spirit.[28] His isolation is
momentary and meaningful, just as Christ goes apart into
the wilderness to commune with God. "Un¡génie est un
accusé,"[29] but even as a solitary he belongs to his people.
Moses is not a suffering, isolated genius but rather the great
leader who guides the Israelites through the wilderness in
quest of the New Canaan. He is an optimistic hero who reflects Hugo's belief in unilinear progress:[30]

Ce qu'il partage, certes, avec son siècle . . . c'est le désir . . . de
découvrir les lois du développement de l'histoire. Cette hantise
. . . est bien le caractère le plus frappant, non seulement de ce
qu'on appelle le romantisme, mais d'un romantisme éternel,
celui auquel se rattachent les "mages" dont Hugo fera le portrait
dans *William Shakespeare*.

Hugo believes that man progresses from barbarism to ever
higher forms of culture despite his momentary setbacks. His
ascent is unilinear, not cyclical.

His belief in unilinear progress is reflected in *La Légende
des siècles,* a record of man's tortuous ascent from primitivism
to civilization. Zumthor discusses the connection of this work
with *La Fin de Satan* and *Dieu:*[31]

L'auteur, du reste, pour compléter ce qu'il a dit plus haut, ne
voit aucune difficulté à faire entrevoir dès à présent qu'il a
esquissé dans la solitude une sorte de poème d'une certaine
étendue où se réverbère le problème unique l'Etre, sous sa triple
face: l'Humanité, le Mal, l'Infini; le progressif, le relatif, l'absolu;
en ce qu'on pourrait appeler trois chants: *La Légende des siècles,
La Fin de Satan, Dieu.*

Hugo is a poet of cultural evolution, and his hero, the poet-
prophet, glimpses into the infinite and then imparts his

knowledge of the Word in order to help society change, develop, progress. The poet-prophet makes man's ultimate victory over nature possible.

Hugo summarizes his attitude in "La Fonction du poète" and "Les Mages." The poet-prophet is inextricably linked to the herd and has a social role, but as a form of higher consciousness he is the head of a sluggish organism which often treats him like an irritant. His feet are planted in this world, his eyes focused upon another. Another intermediary is often necessary—the functionary or enlightened political leader. The hero speaks with God and formulates the maxims by which the functionary may, for example, communicate with the masses. Though the poet-prophet is himself a political leader in antiquity, modern society is more complex and demands a separate functionary. Perhaps it is better, Hugo says, for the poet-prophet not to be overly concerned with social minutiae, which deal after all with the contingent rather than the absolute. He remains a prototype of the Messiah, whom the masses do not understand and rarely love but come to follow in time. The divine Word of which the poet-prophet is the mouthpiece prevails against all force.

Hugo's interest in the poet-prophet as leader prompts him to investigate the nature of poetic communication. He states that the poet-prophet is superior to the herdman because he is suprarational; he has the romantic imagination, a superior mode of understanding. Hugo writes of the poet as priest:[32]

Il y a deux poëtes, le poëte du caprice et le poëte de la logique; et il y a un troisième poëte, composé de l'un et de l'autre, les corrigeant l'un par l'autre, les complétant l'un par l'autre, et les résumant dans une entité plus haute. Ce sont les deux statures en une seule. Ce troisième-là est le premier. Il a le caprice, et il suit le souffle. Il a la logique, et il suit le devoir.

And he says explicitly:[33]

L'imagination est profondeur. Aucune faculté de l'esprit ne s'enfonce et ne creuse plus que l'imagination; c'est la grande plongeuse.

Indeeed imagination is thought,[34] conceived as the immediate comprehension of a visual image without rational analysis. Thought so conceived is suprarational, and discursive interpretation is superfluous. The poet-prophet understands the essence of the thing, and he identifies *thing* with his *idea of the thing* in the appropriate context.

Hugo might well say that in the beginning was the Image, which the poet-prophet brings to mankind in his priestly function. Moreover, the poetic and priestly functions are identical. The Promethean roots are deep, the Moses analogy omnipresent in the concept. Zumthor says of his role as image-bearer:[35]

Dans la contemplation—la vision—de l'univers matériel, l'esprit créateur de Hugo obtient de façon immédiate et, semble-t-il, sans effort, une expression cohérente de cette réalité, expression globale, définitive, parfaitement satisfaisante pour lui parce qu'elle épuise tous les sens qu'il sait donner à l'être—grâce à sa plasticité, à son éclat en même temps qu'à sa valeur philosophique: *image-idée*.

Such an idea of poetic understanding revises some criticism of Hugo. For while critics like Vigny correctly state that he is not an analytic thinker,[36] their judgment is by no means damning. Although Hugo is neither systematic nor very logical, he is nonetheless a thinker because he thinks imaginatively through visual images. Thus Seillière refutes Scherer's assessment:[37]

Il pose tout d'abord que Hugo a peu d'idées et que celles qu'il a restent banales. C'est beaucoup trop dire à mon avis, car, encore une fois, ces idées existent; ce sont toutes celles que le mysticisme naturiste a successivement utilisées pour sa propagande au cours du siècle romantique; Hugo ne les a ni inventées, ni même renouvelées, mais il les a marquées, de sa griffe; elles ont la valeur et la faiblesse rationnelle de toutes les assertions de ce genre. . . .

Hugo simply feels no need for speculative knowledge. The poet-prophet is not a logician who discourses on metaphysical niceties, but rather a romantic hero who mystically encounters reality and then records his experience with the Word for man's benefit.[38] He is both an image-bearer and image-interpreter: "Tout homme qui écrit un livre; ce livre, c'est lui."[39] He is the priest of reality rather than of the Father in Christian theology. He is unique because his imagination penetrates the substance of reality, whereas even the enlightened herdman must rely upon discursive reason. His hypersensibility gives him a capacity beyond the herdman's. He gains knowledge of the Word through his mystical experiences and becomes the leader of his people.

THE VISIONARY

The poet-prophet is always a seer who feels that he either belongs or does not belong to society, that he either is or is not the leader of his people. To some extent he is a visionary. Yet a type of the visionary apart from both the solitary and the leader emerges from the poet-prophet. The visionary is distinguished by his preoccupation with the Word, whereas the solitary and the leader relate the Word to society in social terms. It is a matter of emphasis. Obviously all three types are concerned with the Word and the herd. However, the visionary dwells so much upon the Word and the poetic experience that he tends to forget his audience. He is preoccupied with the message rather than with the people.

The visionary is necessarily concerned with the symbol because it is at the core of the romantic theory of poetic knowledge. He wants to transmute the symbol into the thing. The poem must be more than words, it must be real, it must enable the reader to relive the poet's experience. It must do more than record the visionary's own experience if it is to be meaningful to the reader. The visionary finds himself in a dilemma, for he must necessarily use a language which is inadequate. He despairs of language as an effective means of communication, yet has no other way of transmitting the Word.[40] He must resolve the problem of the poem—a problem in communication which the solitary and the leader ignore.

Assume, for example, that after his mystical experience the

poet-prophet possesses knowledge of the Word. He is still faced with a problem in communication. How will he reveal the Word to others? Several solutions are possible, none altogether satisfactory. He may simply record his knowledge without intending for the reader to relive his experience so that he can experientially derive the poet's understanding of the Word. Vigny takes this approach, and his use of symbolism is representational; he is not a visionary. Hugo and Nerval reject Vigny's approach as unsatisfactory since his symbolism is superficial and does not enable the reader to relive the poet's mystical experience.

In theory Hugo and Nerval resolve this problem of communication in the same way, but their poetry is different because each has a different tone and esthetic approach. They believe, in short, that the symbol is not in one-to-one correspondence with the thing or idea; it has an infinite number of referents. They are not even aware of all the symbol's meanings, but this is no cause for concern. It is, indeed, not necessary for them to understand the *thing* or their experience with the *thing* rationally: It is only necessary for them to record the experience symbolically without a one-to-one correlation of symbol with thing, so that the reader can relive the experience upon reading the poem.

According to this concept of poetry, the symbol introduces the reader to the experience and makes it possible for him to live the experience. Although Hugo and Nerval are not explicit on this point, it may be that no reader can duplicate the poet's own precise experience. Indeed such duplication is unnecessary. The poet wishes to convey the essence of the poetic experience; the reader reacts individually while perceiving the essence of the poet's experience. It is impossible for the reader to have an identical response since he is not the poet. The visionary is nonetheless concerned about these limitations of language. In spite of the open symbol the visionary may not succeed in imparting to the reader his perception of the Word.

Thus the visionary formulates an idea of the open symbol in which symbol=many things=the total experience. Vigny's symbolism is, however, representational: symbol=one specific thing. Although the visionary succeeds in preventing the reader from understanding the poetic experience too narrowly, he is still not satisfied. He can never be certain that his reader will in fact perceive everything or the essence of the thing which he perceives. Language offers no guarantee; the poem is not the thing-in-itself. But the visionary insists that the reader not intellectualize over but actually relive, i.e., create for himself, the experience which originally inspired the poem.

Nerval's visionary is engaged on the quest of the Word, and he seeks an effective mode of revealing it. His search is nebulous because he is preoccupied with the dreamworld, where the dichotomy *reality-ideality* disintegrates and then is fused. The reader relives the experience recorded in the poem and derives his knowledge experientially rather than vicariously. The reader has to derive an understanding experientially because there is no one-to-one correlation of symbol and thing. Since he is not told what the symbol represents and since it indeed represents no one thing, then he must approach the poem as if approaching the thing which the visionary himself originally encounters.

Nerval's world of images and symbols lies in the dreamworld, which the reader, like the visionary, enters and from which he later returns. Nerval characterizes this ethereal world in *Aurélia:*[41]

Le Rêve est une seconde vie. Je n'ai pu percer sans frémir ces portes d'ivoire ou de corne qui nous séparent du monde invisible. Les premiers instants du sommeil sont l'image de la mort; un engourdissement nébuleux saisit notre pensée, et nous ne pouvons déterminer l'instant précis où le *moi,* sous une autre forme, continue l'oeuvre de l'existence. C'est un souterrain vague qui s'éclaire peu à peu, et où se dégagent de l'ombre et de la nuit les pâles figures gravement immobiles qui habitent le séjour des limbes. Puis le tableau se forme, une clarté nouvelle illumine et fait jouer ces apparitions bizarres;—le monde des esprits s'ouvre pour nous.

This scene parallels man's ascent from the cave in Plato's *Republic*, for in both instances man must learn to separate the shadow, the illusion, the image, the symbol from the thing-in-itself. In each case he must come to grips with reality, not the image of reality, but in both instances man is first blinded by the light and fumbles with familiar objects. He is beginning to come into contact with things rather than with the appearances of things. In this sense the dreamworld leads to reality.

Nerval's visionary is hallucinatory and recounts his dreams to the reader. He is not a leader of his people bringing down the commandments from the sacred mountain. In fact, he is so preoccupied with the message that he tends to forget his audience. Yet, ironically, it is his desire to communicate which causes his dissatisfaction with traditional modes of poetic communication and leads him to formulate his own notion.

The symbol is the key because it is more than representational. Through the symbol the reader lives the poetic experience and glimpses the thing; he may go further and glimpse the infinite since the symbol has no limits. It is an open door. Nerval recognizes the danger of such hallucinatory writing:[42]

C'est un entraînement fatal où l'inconnu vous attire comme le feu follet fuyant sur les joncs d'une eau morte. . . . Reprenons pied sur le réel.

The visionary is engaged in the romantic quest of ideality. Moreover ideality is reality—the really real, not the apparently real. In his quest Nerval turns to the dream because it is fluid, imagistic, apparently real like the symbol yet pointing to ideality, reality, the really real. This passage from *Octavie* illustrates his use of the symbol:[43]

Mourir, grand Dieu! pourquoi cette idée me revient-elle à tout propos, comme s'il n'y avait que ma mort qui fût l'équivalent du bonheur que vous promettez? La mort! ce mot ne répand cependant rien de sombre dans ma pensée. Elle m'apparaît couronnée de roses pâles, comme à la fin d'un festin; j'ai rêvé quelquefois qu'elle m'attendait en souriant au chevet d'une femme adorée, après le bonheur, après l'ivresse, et qu'elle me disait: "Allons, jeune homme! tu as eu toute ta part de joie en ce monde. A présent, viens dormir, viens te reposer dans mes bras. Je ne suis pas belle, moi, mais je suis bonne et secourable, et je ne donne pas le plaisir, mais le calme éternel."

The difference between Nerval's use of symbolism and Vigny's is striking. Vigny's symbol is static, representational; Nerval's kinetic, kaleidoscopic. It contains the manifold possibilities of the poetic experience itself.

Hugo's use of the symbol is similar in theory but different in practice. This difference becomes apparent by contrasting two poems, Hugo's "La Conscience" and Nerval's "Capharnaum," in which both writers treat the effect of man's conscience upon himself. In "La Conscience" the great eye, symbolizing conscience, ceaselessly follows the sinner, Caïn, through the world, affording no rest, arising whenever Caïn believes he has it. In "La Capharnaum"[44] the symbol is open: The poet walks up and down staircases, back and forth along never-ending corridors, while slushing black waters produce eerie sensations. The entire scene, rather than a part of it, symbolizes man punished by conscience for his transgressions. Both Hugo and Nerval are imagistic, but there is much difference. Hugo's symbol is marmoreal, Nerval's plastic; Hugo achieves his effect through a particular symbol though it is not representational, while Nerval uses the entire scene as a symbol. The following equation is valid for Hugo— image=thought=symbol=the Word. In Nerval such an equation is impossible because the symbol is too uncertain. He intimates that image leads to symbol and symbol to the Word. He emphasizes the multiplicity of referents by not symbolizing the Word in one image. Indeed, the fundamental ambiguity in life precludes such a marmoreal use of the symbol:[45]

Ici a commencé pour moi ce que j'appellerai l'épanchement du songe dans la vie réelle. A dater de ce moment, tout prenait parfois un aspect double,—et cela, sans que le raisonnement manquât jamais de logique, sans que la mémoire perdît les plus légers détails de ce qui m'arrivait. Seulement, mes actions, insensées en apparence, étaient soumises à ce qu'on appelle l'illusion, selon la raison humaine.

These lines from *Aurélia* underscore his distrust of language, a basic distrust which extends to the symbol.

Words never capture the essence of the thing. Michaud depicts this aspect of the pre-symbolist mind:[46]

Comment atteindrait-il donc l'objet de ses rêves, lui qui renie à la fois le dogme et la raison, lui qui ne reconnaît plus pour valable, par une réaction naturelle, mais excessive, que la voix du seul sentiment? Car là est bien le drame romantique. En soi, le Romantique a raison de vouloir dépasser le norme classique, et d'étendre, pour ainsi dire, la notion de la perfection du fini à l'infini.

In the dream and poem, as in life, the visionary perceives his own perception while the thing-in-itself remains elusive. Perhaps the thing, like the name Jehovah for the ancient Israelites, is too sacred for human knowledge; one comes closest to it through the symbol. Yet there is an escape. Although the visionary may not understand reality in its totality, he can have a vision of it.[47] And he can symbolically transfigure this vision into a poem which causes the reader to have a similar vision.

"Artémis" is such a visionary poem. It in no way corresponds to reality, but it synthesizes the dreams and hallucinations of *Aurélia* and transfigures reality. The visionary's imagistic impression is, at length, the road to the Image itself. Nerval's hero descends like Orpheus into the abyss "pour y puiser l'inspiration,"[48] then returns with a vision of the Image. He describes his vision, knowing the essence of the thing is unfathomable. Perhaps symbolism replaces romanticism at this point. In comparison Hugo is less sophisticated, for he communes with God and then returns to earth with a vision of the image equated with the thing, the message, the Word. Nerval's visionary maintains that the symbol can only lead to the thing, that the poet perceives reality distortedly—the best the hero can do. And he can only hope that the reader will glimpse reality by reliving the symbolically recorded experience.

SUMMARY

Perhaps Van Tieghem best summarizes the contributions of Baudelaire, Vigny, Hugo, and Nerval to the concept of the poet-prophet:[49]

Si l'art donne des droits à l'individu qui a du génie, il lui impose des devoirs; l'artiste n'est plus moralement libre qu'en artiste; chose curieuse, la liberté que tous les romantiques ont réclamée pour la technique de l'oeuvre d'art, ils y renoncent d'eux-mêmes en ce qui concerne son but. Tous, à partir de 1830, se croient, à part Gautier et Musset, chargés d'une mission non pas morale, mais sociale, et humanitaire. Egalement éloignés de la propagande morale sour le prétexte de laquelle nos classiques feignaient d'écrire, de "l'art pour l'art" qui sera de mode à partir de 1850, et de l'action politique directe que condamnera un Vigny dans *La Maison du berger,* le romantisme de 1830-1840 prétend, "les pieds ici, la tête ailleurs," diriger les peuples vers un avenir meilleur; cette prétention suppose une philosophie, ou une conception du monde au nom de laquelle le poète parlera et qu'il s'efforcera de faire triompher, ou tout au moins de faire connaître; elle suppose aussi que le poète, qui n'est pas qu'un porte-parole, est lui-même éclairé par une inspiration que ne reçoivent pas les autres hommes; à son don d'expression, à sa possibilité d'influence, qu'ils voient supérieure à ceux des autres écrivains, s'ajoute le don de visionnaire dont le gratifie la puissance céleste.

Thus the poet-prophet, a descendant of the divine *vates,* thinks he must use his unusual powers for man's benefit. He has both the awareness and romantic sensibility which characterize the archetypal self-conscious hero; indeed he would not be the poet-prophet without these two qualities. No less than three types of the poet-prophet emerge from his concern with the Word and the herd—the solitary, the leader, the visionary. The lines are indefinite, they sometimes cross, but the poet-prophet always feels he is unique. He believes he knows more and feels more deeply than other men, and he is necessarily concerned with both his audience and the poetic message. He may be so concerned with one that he tends to forget the other. The visionary, unlike the leader, is so blinded by the revelation of the Word that in his ecstasy he tends to forget the people for whom the mystical message is intended.

FIVE

THE REBEL AND THE DANDY

THE romantic rebel personifies defiance. A caricature might well depict him as a superman standing upon a promontory during a storm and shaking his fist at God, or as a lonely genius convinced he is much too fine for this earth, or as a scornful dandy sullied by the people around him. And such a caricature stresses his basic trait—egotism.

Fundamentally the rebel is an egotist or an egomaniac. He epitomizes individuality and his self-assertion inevitably results in his conflict with society. While he may be no more than a blind egocentric force, he most often rebels consciously against the laws of society and/or God. Indeed this is his nature—the assertion of self against an outside force. He may rebel in one of three ways—against the cosmos or God as a metaphysical rebel, against society as a social rebel, or against both as a fusion of the two types. The second kind of rebellion becomes metaphysical if the hero visualizes society as divinely ordained or as a reflection of the cosmic order. The third type, the fusion, is best illustrated by the dandy, who closely resembles the rebel in fiction but who differs somewhat in theory.

The rebel acts from one of several motives. He may be an

imp of the perverse and his rebelliousness a kind of nihilism. Or if he believes that the social laws are immoral, he may develop a new source of law to replace the traditional code. He brings a different code to mankind, or at least he himself acts according to a different code which he recommends for mankind. The rebel feels that the universe is out of joint, and he often lashes out against either God or the cosmic order. He is "lawless" in refuting the laws of God and man; in time he becomes a "criminal." And while it is society which calls him a criminal in its value-judgment, the rebel sometimes considers himself a criminal. Thus there are delicate shadings and subtypes in the concept of the romantic rebel. However, he must fundamentally be either a social rebel, a metaphysical rebel, or a fusion of the two, like the dandy.

The Social Rebel

The social rebel is rooted in the noble savage, an early romantic conception of the ideal man. As Weil observes, Chateaubriand poses a dichotomy of savage-European in which the rebel, the outsider, the savage, is good, and the European always evil:[1]

Cette antithèse fondamentale du Sauvage et de l'Européen, de "l'homme des forêts" et de "l'homme des cités," trahit assez l'influence de J.-J. Rousseau et rattache Chateaubriand à une tradition. . . . Il déclare en 1797: "Délivré du joug tyrannique de la société, je compris alors les charmes de cette indépendance de la nature, qui surpassent de bien loin tous les plaisirs dont l'homme civil peut avoir l'idée. Je compris pourquoi un Sauvage ne s'est pas fait Européen, et pourquoi plusieurs Européens se sont fait sauvages. . . .

This is an explicit attack upon the social institutions of Europe. Chateaubriand believes the savage is right in obeying natural laws rather than European mores because the latter are unnatural. Thus René is a rebel who turns from an unjust society to one which harmonizes with natural justice and law. By praising man's natural state the early romantics make an implicit criticism of European society. These men, like Bernardin de Saint-Pierre, are in a direct line from Rousseau, an early rebel. Like Chateaubriand's their attack is sometimes explicit, sometimes implicit, but at this time a concept of the hero as a rebel awaits definitive treatment. It awaits, indeed, a clear expression of the romantic ego as it motivates rebelliousness.

Hernani asserts himself egotistically and rebels against society. He attacks the King who murdered his father and robbed him of his inheritance; the revenge-motif motivates Hernani's assault upon the ruling order. But it is not *society* which he attacks. Though proscribed by the King he is not a criminal. Yet he is aware of a lawless element in his character:[2]

> Je suis une force qui va!
> Agent aveugle et sourd de mystères funèbres!
> Une âme de malheur faite avec des ténèbres!
> Où vais-je? je ne sais. Mais je me sens poussé
> D'un souffle impétueux, d'un destin insensé.
> Je descends, je descends, et jamais ne m'arrête.
> Si parfois, haletant, j'ose tourner la tête,
> Une voix me dit: Marche! et l'abîme est profond,
> Et de flamme ou de sang je le vois rouge au fond!
> Cependant, à l'entour de ma course farouche,
> Tout se brise, tout meurt. Malheur à qui me touche!
> Oh! fuis! détourne-toi de mon chemin fatal,
> Hélas! sans le vouloir, je te ferais du mal!

Such lawlessness is a blind, egotistical force, but it is not criminality. Its stated purpose is self-assertion, not the overthrow of specific religious or social laws. Hernani rebels, because of his principle of disorder, against the King who wrongs him; even without the revenge-motif his lawlessness would remain since it proceeds naturally from his egotism. He is fighting a particular King, a ruling order, not the essence or structure of society abstractly conceived. This distinguishes him from other rebels who are in fact warring against society.

Hernani stands "immobile . . . dans l'ombre, les bras

isés sous le long manteau qui l'enveloppe, et le large bord
son chapeau relevé,"³ bristling with indignation. His fa-
ty is related to his rebelliousness, for his rebellious self-
rtion sets into motion a relentless chain of cause and effect
society. His egotism governs his actions. It motivates him
the "force qui va" and accounts for his lawlessness. His
rebelliousness is rooted in his egotism.

Julien Sorel is a different kind of egotist. He is ambitious
in a world of brutal egotists in Stendhal's *Le Rouge et le
noir*. He believes that most men mask their egotism with
conformity in an effort to achieve their goal. Although there
is a spirit of rebelliousness in all men, the successful egotist
disguises it. Every man is essentially an anarchist since he is
at war with society, but the clever man wages this war by
subterfuge. He must profess to accept the precepts of society
in order to manipulate its laws to his own advantage. All
men are egotistic and to that extent rebellious; only some
are more successful than others:⁴

Que je suis bon, se dit-il, moi, plébéien, avoir pitié d'une famille
de ce rang! Moi, que le duc de Chaulnes appelle un domestique!
Comment le marquis augmente-t-il son immense fortune? En
vendant de la rente, quand il apprend au Château qu'il y aura
le lendemain apparence de coup d'Etat. Et moi, jeté au dernier
rang par une Providence marâtre, moi à qui elle a donné un
coeur noble et pas mille francs de rente. . . . Une source limpide
qui vient étancher ma soif dans le désert brûlant de la médio-
crité que je traverse si péniblement! Ma foi, pas si bête; chacun
pour soi dans ce désert d'égoïsme qu'on appelle la vie.

Since the egotist slyly manipulates society to his benefit, it
follows that he must be a hypocrite. He is indeed a social
rebel, and his ambition results, as with Sorel, in this rebelliousness. Sorel differs from the bourgeoisie only by doing
what they dream of, and from the aristocracy by beating
them at their own game of hypocrisy. He is a titan of selfishness, ambition, egotism; he is a rebel. He early determines to
assert himself and to find a place in the sun, and he pursues
this course of action irrespective of cost. He rebels by covert-

ly opposing all social laws, he observes no moral laws but his own, and his egotism ultimately results in his social revolt.

Dumas *père's* Antony is a social rebel. As a superior man he hypersensitively rebels against a society which condemns him for his illegitimacy. Adèle describes him to her friend Clara:[5]

Oh, si tu l'avais suivi comme moi au milieu du monde, où il semblait étranger, parce qu'il lui était supérieur; si tu l'avais vu triste et sévère au milieu de ces jeunes fous, élégants et nuls.

Society is unjust and cruel. He cannot marry Adèle because he has no station in life. Although he rebels he cannot win against a formidable, impersonal enemy like society. He leaves Adèle without explanation, and he mysteriously returns years later. His behavior continues to be erratic; he even wounds himself in order to stay in her house and have a chance to gain first her sympathy then her love. He recounts his life and reveals his love. Finally he carries her away although he knows they cannot evade society. Then, always following his own code rather than society's, he kills Adèle to protect her reputation, ironically, in the corrupt society which condemns him.

Balzac's Eugène de Rastignac is a successful Julien Sorel. Society makes a rebel of him because at first Rastignac, unlike Sorel, is an idealist who feels that man can obtain the place he merits in the world. Balzac's implicit theme is that a good man will inevitably be destroyed by an unjust society. Of course, the rebel is one who does not act according to the established code; but since few men believe the code they profess and would in fact be destroyed if they did, then all men—certainly all successful men—are rebels. There are two societies, the real and the apparent, and there are two kinds of rebels. One kind, the criminal like Vautrin, wars against the social precepts, but the other, like Rastignac, manipulates the apparently real code in order to succeed in the real society. Both men are rebels but they express themselves differently.

Consider Rastignac's career. The facts of his life are simple. A young man, the son of impoverished nobility, comes to Paris in 1819 to study law. He lives in the Pension Vauquer, where he comes to know diverse types of Parisians and where he meets Vautrin, the notorious Jacques Collin of the Paris underworld. His naïveté and idealism contrast sharply with Vautrin's cynical wisdom. Rastignac becomes in time Mme de Nucingen's lover—one of Old Goriot's daughters. He is sickened, however, by the way she and her sister abuse their father.

Rastignac's egotism grows under the guise of ambition in *Le Père Goriot*. Vautrin tells him:[6]

Avoir de l'ambition, mon petit coeur, ce n'est pas donné à tout le monde. Demandez aux femmes quels hommes elles recherchent, les ambitieux. Les ambitieux ont les reins plus forts, le sang plus riche en fer, le coeur plus chaud que ceux des autres hommes.

But honest ambition, he hastens to add, does not bear fruit:[7]

L'honnêteté ne sert à rien. L'on plie sous le pouvoir du génie, on le hait, on tâche de le calomnier, parce qu'il prend sans partager. La corruption est en force.

Rastignac has ample opportunity to see corruption. It is significant that though he refuses to marry the wealthy girl Vautrin chooses for him in *Le Père Goriot*, he frankly pursues an Alsatian for her money, years later, in *Peau de chagrin*. His idealism dies by degrees, his cynicism grows steadily, and once matured he is a formidable rebel. He consciously enunciates rebellion as a philosophy in the closing scene of *Le Père Goriot*. Accompanied by Christophe, he buries Old Goriot, whose daughters are not present though he gave both his money and life for them. With their bestial ingratitude in mind Rastignac muses in one of Balzac's most striking scenes:[8]

Rastignac, resté seul, fit quelques pas vers le haut du cimetière et vit Paris tortueusement couché le long des deux rives de la Seine, où commençaient à briller les lumières. Ses yeux s'attachèrent presque avidement entre la colonne de la place Vendôme et le dôme des Invalides, là où vivait ce beau monde dans lequel il avait voulu pénétrer. Il lança sur cette ruche bourdonnante un regard qui semblait par avance en pomper le miel, et dit ces mots grandioses: "A nous deux maintenant!"

Et pour premier acte de défi qu'il portait à la société, Rastignac alla dîner chez Madame de Nucingen.

Vautrin has counseled well, and Rastignac becomes a good student. He is ready to confront and manipulate society. He has become a prototype of the successful rebel—the hypocrite.

THE METAPHYSICAL REBEL

The metaphysical rebel is also an egotist. He incarnates the spirit of nihilism and lawlessness, and as with Lucifer it is the ego, pride, which causes him to challenge divine law. He may also seek to replace the old law with the new or supersede the old by a new interpretation of it. As a Promethean rebel he may attempt to discover the forbidden secrets of the universe. Yet whatever his distinguishing characteristic, the rebel is an egotist and his rebellion springs from egotism.

The influence of the Byronic hero is great; indeed Byronism is synonymous with overweening pride. Byronism has both social and metaphysical roots, but the former are best understood in terms of the latter. The Byronic hero is satanic on the metaphysical plane even as he egotistically lashes out against society. Estève, in studying Byron's impact upon French romanticism, comments upon the contiguity of the social and metaphysical revolt:[9]

Le byronisme, c'est la révolte de l'individu contre la société, mais c'est aussi la révolte de l'homme contre la vie. L'un est d'ailleurs la conséquence de l'autre.

The French romantics regard Byron as the principle of satanic pride, lawlessness, spiritual inquietude, thirst for knowledge—all rebellious traits on the metaphysical plane. Byron is Manfred incarnate, the solitary brooding high in the uninhabited mountains, and in league with the devil. He makes an indelible imprint upon French romanticism.

The Byronic rebel has a metaphysical purpose; he wants to discover the secrets of the universe. In his quest of forbidden knowledge he gears his sensibility to intolerable heights in order to enjoy acuter perception. The danger is apparent:[10]

Les sensibilités surexcitées exigent une réponse immédiate: elles s'irritent de ne pouvoir l'obtenir. De là le malaise des âmes, déchirées par le conflit de la raison et du coeur, également incapables de retourner à la foi ancienne et de s'en créer une nouvelle; de là les doutes, les angoisses, les aspirations confuses, contradictoires, qui se répercuteront en plaintes éloquentes ou en cris sublimes dans la poésie du XIXe siècle.

When he does not obtain an answer, the hero becomes destructive—the fatal man—and acts on the social as well as the metaphysical plane. The Byronic rebel possesses the fatal gift of genius and tends to merge with the poet-prophet as well as with the fatal man. The rebel is complex and has many facets, but above all he is the spirit of energy expressed lawlessly in revolt.

Satan as a rebel is a theme in Lamartine, Vigny, and Hugo. Lamartine portrays him sympathetically in *La Chute d'un ange*. Vigny projects a solution to the metaphysical problem of rebellion by reconciling him with God in *Satan sauvé*. Although satanism is sometimes a pose, it more often reflects the writer's concern with free will and man's place in the cosmos. It deals with the hero's relationship to society and God. Zumthor observes, for instance, that Hugo uses Satan as a pivotal symbol:[11]

Dans la trilogie achevée, *La Fin de Satan,* formant un centre de la composition, aurait eu en particulier pour but d'établir le contact entre les parties plus éloignées de l'oeuvre, la *Légende* et *Dieu*—entre le relatif présent, pour ainsi parler, à l'état pur, et *l'absolu* dans sa transcendance. Elle devait montrer comment ils coexistent, comment ils réagissent l'un sur l'autre—et dans quelle mesure on peut dire qu'ils sont identiques. Elle constituait le moment unique, l'instance poétique où le temps devient capable d'absorber l'éternité.

Thus satanism is often a quest for the infinite rather than a cult of perversity. At least in Hugo an equation Satan=rebel =hero may be drawn:[12]

Dans les personnes: c'est parce qu'il en est une que Satan peut être sauvé. Il reste vrai néanmoins que, si l'équation Satan= Hugo=l'Homme a permis au poète, dans la mesure où elle répondait à une profonde exigence de son esprit, d'atteindre à un lyrisme poignant, elle touche de fort près à l'allégorie.

This allegory concerns the satanic rebel's relationship to God. Egotistic rebelliousness or pride motivates his insurrection; thus reconciliation and atonement are the poet's concern.

The satanic rebel is neither happy with his fate nor satisfied with himself. He is invariably a melancholy man as in Vigny's *Eloa,* and unlike the later decadent attitude romanticism characterizes him as a tragic hero profoundly aware of former glory and present anguish. He takes no pleasure in his revolt:[13]

"Où me conduisez-vous, bel Ange?—Viens toujours.
—Que votre voix est triste, et quel sombre discours.
N'est-ce pas Eloa qui soulève ta chaîne?
J'ai cru t'avoir sauvé.—Non, c'est moi qui t'entraîne.
—Si nous sommes unis, peu m'importe en quel lieu!
Nomme-moi donc encore ou ta Soeur ou ton Dieu!
—J'enlève mon esclave et je tiens ma victime.
—Tu paraissais si bon! Oh! qu'ai-je fait?—Un crime.
—Seras-tu plus heureux du moins, es-tu content?
—Plus triste que jamais.—Qui donc es-tu?—Satan.

Both Satan and the *Deus absconditus* are figures in the Christian worldview. Satan is titanic even as a pale hero; he is monumental as a hero of solitude and suffering. The egotist incarnates the will in his metaphysical rebellion against God. Vigny's problem is to allow Satan, i.e., the hero as rebel, his measure of self-assertion and individualism, yet somehow effect a reconciliation with God. And it is quite a task.

In "La Révolte" from *Les Fleurs du mal* Baudelaire

introduces three rebels, Saint Peter, Cain, and Satan. He
visualizes God as a tyrant who demands unquestioning obedience from his children. Rebelliousness is inevitable in this
setting; it evolves from the hero's individualism.

Baudelaire says there are two antipodal groups of men—
the races of Cain and Abel. They have fought since God first
showed his preference for Abel, thus provoking Cain to slay
his brother. He says, furthermore, that Cain and his descendants have been wronged; Abel and his children are
favorites because they are subservient. They have surren-
dered something of themselves, and Abel reaps the harvest
because he fawns before God the tyrannical Father. On the
other hand, must Cain wallow in the mud because he retains
his integrity? Must his descendants consequently be ill-kept,
persecuted, cursed? Baudelaire exclaims:[14]

> Race d'Abel, voici ta honte:
> Le fer est vaincu par l'épieu!
>
> Race de Caïn, au ciel monte,
> Et sur la terre jette Dieu!

Here as elsewhere he aligns himself with the rebel. In "Le
Reniement de Saint Pierre" Baudelaire writes:[15]

> —Certes, je sortirai, quant à moi, satisfait
> D'un monde où l'action n'est pas la soeur du rêve;
> Puissé-je user du glaive et périr par le glaive!
> Saint Pierre a renié Jésus. . . il a bien fait!

He pays homage to the principle of negation. His diabolism
represents his identification with Satan as the metaphysical
rebel, the egotistical hero who asserts his will against God's
law.

Since self-assertion is pride, the cardinal sin, Lucifer as
the incarnation of pride is the first great rebel and the
archetype for all who follow. It is therefore natural that
Baudelaire prays to Satan for aid and knowledge in "Les
Litanies de Satan." By an inverted logic there is nothing
impious in his prayer, for the poem portrays God as the

obstinate tyrant who peevishly demands obedience from his children. Egotism is identified with individualism and self-assertion—good romantic virtues. Thus Satan, like Cain, is unjustly punished by a tyrant. Baudelaire prays:[16]

> Gloire et louange à toi, Satan, dans les hauteurs
> Du Ciel, où tu régnas, et dans les profondeurs
> De l'Enfer, où, vaincu, tu rêves en silence!
> Fais que mon âme un jour, sous l'Arbre de Science,
> Près de toi se repose, à l'heure où sur ton front
> Comme un Temple nouveau ses rameaux s'épandront.

The romantic hero follows Satan as the archetypal rebel, just as the fallen angels fight for him in heaven. The rebel's pride leads ultimately to criminality; it is the taint of original sin. Since egotism is natural, it follows that man is natural when he is egotistic and when he asserts himself against the tyrant's law.

Consequently Baudelaire, as an orthodox Christian, disapproves of what is natural for man just as he simultaneously testifies to its appeal and power. Man's *natural* state, his *nature,* is corrupt, and the hero as a metaphysical rebel is evil. He must change his nature, he must deny himself, for otherwise he cannot be reconciled with God the Father. Thus Baudelaire's diabolism fits neatly into an orthodox Christian worldview.

Han d'Islande exemplifies the metaphysical rebel in Hugo's novel of the same name. Hans of Iceland rebels against God, i.e., the principle of love and harmony, as he acts in society. He rebels as a manic killer while Count Ahlefeld rebels against Danish rule in Northern Norway. The plot-structure is complex, although it turns in general upon the Trondheim miners' insurrection and Hans's bitter hatred of life. Hugo implicitly contrasts the social and metaphysical aspects of the rebel. Count Ahlefeld and the miners are social rebels as they fight to cast off Danish occupation, and Hans of Iceland is a metaphysical rebel as he kills with nihilistic joy. His supposed motive—avenging his son, Gill Stadt—is spurious.

His love of destruction and death is the real motive.

Hans reveals his true nature at the trial when he confesses that he is the real Hans of Iceland and surrenders because he is tired of killing; he turns his deathwish in upon himself. He states in the crowded courtroom: "Ma nature est de haïr les hommes, ma mission de leur nuire."[17] He elaborates further after he is thrust into prison with Schumacker. Hugo differentiates between the social and metaphysical rebels as the two men look at each other in silence, recognizing they are both enemies of man:[18]

—Qui es-tu? demande enfin l'ex-chancelier au brigand.
—. . . Han d'Islande.
—. . . Je t'aime parce que tu hais les hommes.
—Voilà pourquoi je te hais.
—Ecoute, je hais les hommes, comme toi, parce que je leur ai fait du bien, et qu'ils m'ont fait du mal.
—Tu ne les hais pas comme moi; je les hais, moi, parce qu'ils m'ont fait du bien, et que je leur ai rendu du mal.

Then Hans recounts the story of his life, and he describes the ecstasy of sadistic murder:[19]

—Le bonheur de sentir des chairs palpitantes frémir sous ma dent, un sang fumant réchauffer mon gosier altéré; la volupté de briser des êtres vivants contre des pointes de rochers, et d'entendre le cri de la victime se mêler au bruit des membres fracassés. Voilà les plaisirs que m'ont procuré les hommes.

He is of course a nihilist; he destroys because he has an abstract hatred of life. Since men are the concrete expressions of life, he feels that he somehow subtracts from the universal principle with each murder he commits. Yet his task is ultimately impossible because he cannot kill everyone. Moreover, he has no son to carry on his work as he has inherited his mission from his father and grandfather. In short, he is doomed to failure because he has no satisfactory weapon to use against the object of his wrath. He is a metaphysical rebel acting in a social context. He never reaches the object of his rebellion—life and the cosmos.

The Fusion: The Dandy

Hans of Iceland is a metaphysical rebel acting on the social plane, but this is not what is meant by the fusion. Hans and the other heroes so far studied share a common trait: They act in relationship to something; they have an adversary, an object of opposition, which is society and/or God. The categories are, of course, not always separate. The metaphysical rebel, like Hans of Iceland, acts in the social context because he cannot destroy an abstraction. Furthermore it is impossible, as Baudelaire and Vigny say, for him to win a war against an omnipotent God. In brief, both social and metaphysical rebels are subjects who act in relation to an object, an adversary.

However, it is different with the dandy, who represents a fusion of the social and metaphysical aspects. His egomania is such that in theory, though not always in practice, he acts only in relation to himself; as a subject he is unconcerned about an object, an adversary. He does not rebel against God or man in theory, for neither is worth the trouble and both are beneath his dignity. Yet if social and divine laws exist— and society believes they do—then the dandy is necessarily related to them, even though he does not rebel against either. He cannot act out of context or in a vacuum.

The dandy is simply asserting himself, and if God or society should get in his way, so much the worse for them. But in theory he does not oppose them, at least not consciously; and conscious rebellion is what defines the rebel as a type of the self-conscious hero. In this respect the dandy is neither a social nor a metaphysical rebel. But since he belongs to a society and one, moreover, which has an accepted idea of God, then he has to act in relationship to them. A social or cosmic vacuum manifestly does not exist. Thus the dandy is a fusion of both the social and metaphysical rebels in actuality, even though not in theory. Evaluative standards applied to them must also assess the dandy because they are the standards of judgment inherent in the very structure of society. Moreover, some dandies do not act according to theory. In

France, particularly, they are quite conscious of their rebellion against society and God.

The dandy is a romantic hero because he is a titan—or at least wishes to be after his fashion. According to Clement, titanism is one characteristic of the romantic spirit:[20]

Romanticism wants everything, action, passions, character, setting, on a large scale. Accordingly titanism is one of its traits. Titanism is bred out of disenchantment, disillusionment, and satiety. The romantic character is blasé. . . .

Certainly this description fits the dandy. He is indeed a disenchanted titan, and when he sins he sins on a colossal scale. He is not only evil but the incarnation of evil; Barbey's dandies are, for instance, satisfied with nothing less. But this is the dandy from a social viewpoint; he would, in theory, find the adjectives quite meaningless. For the dandy is unique as he epitomizes rebelliousness in his rolé as the great egomaniac.

Dandyism is a worldview which Barbey defines:[21]

Le Dandysme est toute une manière d'être, et l'on n'est pas que par le côté matériellement visible. C'est une manière d'être, entièrement composée de nuances, comme il arrive toujours dans les sociétés très vieilles et très civilisées, où la comédie devient si rare et où la convenance triomphe à peine de l'ennui.

Dandyism is a worldview characterized by a distinct attitude towards the romantic sensibility. The dandy does not wish to reveal his emotions. He is in fact a man of sensibility, but his emotional revels enervate him and leave him in a state of perpetual boredom so that spleen and ennui are his invariable reactions. In theory, though not in practice, he always acts in response to himself.

No other dandy in history or fiction captures the imagination more than the supreme egomaniac, the archetype, George Bryan Brummell. Barbey describes him:[22]

Il vécut de pair à compagnon avec toutes les puissances, toutes les supériorités de son époque, et, par l'aisance, il s'éleva jusqu'à leur niveau. Où de plus habiles se seraient perdus, il se sauvait. Son audace était de la justesse. Il pouvait toucher impunément à la hache. On a dit pourtant que cette hache, dont il avait tant de fois défié le tranchant, le coupa enfin: qu'il intéressa à sa perte la vanité d'un Dandy comme lui, d'un Dandy royal, S. M. Georges IV; mais son empire avait été si grand que, s'il avait voulu, il l'eût repris.

But his ego does not permit him to ask even a King's pardon, for he is ever too proud to show his emotions. He regards a display of emotions as vulgar emotionalism. Subtlety is his keynote.

The dandy is isolated by his egomaniac self-preoccupation. Baudelaire describes him in "Don Juan aux enfers":[23]

> Tout droit dans son armure, un grand homme de pierre
> Se tenait à la barre et coupa le flot noir;
> Mais le calme héros, courbé sur sa rapière,
> Regardait le sillage et ne daignait rien voir.

He is typically conscious of himself and unconscious of the world. Yet as he acts self-assertively, he tends to be destructive and so he may be accounted a rebel. He rebels simply by refusing to recognize social and moral laws. Canu discusses the relationship of Brummell's vanity and sensibility, and his remarks apply to any dandy as he acts egotistically:[24]

Son génie fut d'étendre cette religion de la réserve savante et exclusive, du costume à l'allure, à la tenue, aux usages mondains, à la conservation, aux sentiments mêmes. Un dandy digne de ce nom se doit d'être étranger aux menues affections des simples mortels, à la colère, au dépit, à la cupidité, à la curiosité, à la souffrance, à la pitié, à l'amour même. Il ne veut rien savoir de ces misères, ou du moins il n'en montre rien. Ainsi se développe en lui la vanité d'être différent, d'être supérieur, et de ne pas le manifester autrement qu'en le dissimulant. On imagine les jouissances perverses que peuvent donner ces voluptés solitaires. Brummell leur dut son incroyable ascendant.

His external trimmings, like his finery and cold, haughty demeanor, form a protective armor against the world. With such a weapon he can afford to ignore society and the cosmos because neither can harm him.

Clement summarizes the dandy's psychology:[25]

At bottom, dandyism was a sort of *frenzy to be different,* not only in externals, but psychologically as well, sprung from the ennui that oppressed the generations of the first half of the nineteenth century.

He is indeed unique and acts accordingly. He observes only his own laws, and if in observing them he flouts social or religious precepts, he is not aware of it or at least he is not concerned. He is, however, a fusion of the metaphysical and social rebels, for his self-assertion inevitably results in moral and social conflict. The fact of this conflict remains nonetheless true even if in theory he is not trying to change society or opposing the order of things.

Such is the theoretical basis of the dandy, but practice has a way of differing from theory. While some dandies conform to the concept of the ideal dandy, others consciously rebel and flout society and the moral law in every conceivable way. Social protest is necessarily a strong theme.

Both kinds of dandies are present in Barbey's *Les Diaboliques.* For example, Captain Brassard of "Le Rideau cramoisi" ignores the social and moral laws. He despises emotion and relates his story to the interlocutor, who thus describes him:[26]

Il se tut encore, ce dandy qui m'avait raconté, sans le moindre dandysme, une histoire d'une si triste réalité. Je rêvais sous l'impression de cette histoire, et je comprenais que ce brillant vicomte de Brassard, la fleur non des *pois,* mais des plus fiers pavots rouges du dandysme, le buveur grandiose de *claret,* à la manière anglaise, fût comme un autre, un homme plus profond qu'il ne paraissait.

It is of course not the dandy, Captain Brassard, who changes during the story but rather the skeptic, who for the first time realizes that the dandy is profounder than he seems. In this instance, at least, the dandy is more than a fop, a flippant rebel.

In "Le Bonheur dans le crime" the rebel, Savigny, ignores the social and moral laws. He and his mistress, Hauteclaire, poison his wife. Dr. Torty, whom Mme de Savigny tells of the crime on her deathbed, promises her to remain silent in order to preserve the family name from dishonor, but he scruti-- nizes the Comte and Hauteclaire during the ensuing years. He frankly hopes for their remorse, repentance, discovery, damnation, but is at last compelled to admit:[27]

Cette boue d'un crime lâche qui n'avait pas eu le courage d'être sanglant, je n'en ai pas une seule fois aperçu la tache sur l'azur de leur bonheur! C'est à terrasser, n'est-il pas vrai? tous les moralistes de la terre, qui ont inventé un bel axiome du vice puni et de la vertu récompensée! Abandonnés et solitaires comme ils l'étaient, ne voyant que moi, avec lequel ils ne se gênaient plus qu'avec un médecin devenu presque un ami, à force de hantises, ils ne se surveillaient point.

Savigny and Hauteclaire are not conscious of transgressing the moral code; they simply ignore it. The traits of the dandy as a kind of ideal rebel are present—his egotistic self-affirmation and utter obliviousness of the social and moral law.

The dandies of "A un Dîner d'athées" are however very different. They are conscious of society and indeed take delight in affronting the herdmen. As atheists they make a fetish of rebelling against the divine law. One dandy speaks of "l'égoïsme, l'*inexilable* égoïsme, que l'art du monde est de voiler sous des formes aimables. . . ."[28] This sort of dandy resembles the herdman in one respect. He does not evidence the grand unconcern of the ideal dandy, and he is in fact rather petty as he tries to shock the *bon bourgeois*. His re- belliousness is socially and metaphysically oriented, he has objects for his egotistic expression, and thus he is radically different from the ideal dandy.

Hence there are two types of the dandy as rebel—the ideal man who, as his own subject and object, is unconcerned with moral and social law, and the dandy as a cultural product acting against a social or divine adversary. Canu notes the difference:[29]

Mais il ne s'agissait pas là d'un modèle à imiter en tout point. Barbey en retient surtout l'idée maîtresse, qui répond d'ailleurs à la tradition française du courtisan de Louis XIV et du héros classique: sembler maître de soi, ne trahir par sa mise comme par sa conduite, aucun attachement particulier, telle est la meilleure méthode pour dominer les autres, ou, au minimu, éviter leur emprise. . . . Le dandysme français . . . s'accommode mal du calme et de la discrétion de son aîné d'Outre-Manche. Il s'accompagne de plus en plus d'une provocation aux conventions bourgeoises, d'habitudes insolentes et dévergondées.

When he begins deliberately to provoke the bourgeois, the dandy becomes of course a social rebel. He is no longer the ideal man.

In "Le Peintre de la vie moderne" Baudelaire discusses the difference between theory and practice. He says that in theory the dandy uses his romantic sensibility to make a cult of himself. He is really the ideal man:[30]

C'est avant tout le besoin ardent de se faire une originalité, contenu dans les limites extérieures des convenances. C'est une espèce de culte de soi-même, qui peut survivre à la recherche du bonheur à trouver dans autrui, dans la femme, par exemple; qui peut survivre même à tout ce qu'on appelle les illusions. C'est le plaisir d'étonner et la satisfaction orgueilleuse de ne jamais être étonné. Un dandy peut être un homme blasé, peut être un homme souffrant; mais, dans ce dernier cas, il sourira comme le Lacédémonien sous la morsure du renard.

The dandy must live up to his ideal of himself—one which of course precludes a prosaic wish to reform society. Yet in the same essay Baudelaire correctly observes that dandies are characterized by social protest. In short they are different in practice from what they are in theory:[31]

Que ces hommes se fassent nommer raffinés, incroyables, beaux, lions ou dandys, tous sont issus d'une même origine; tous participent du même caractère d'opposition et de révolte; tous sont des représentants de ce qu'il y a de meilleur dans l'orgueil humain, de ce besoin, trop rare chez ceux d'aujourd'hui, de combattre et de détruire la trivialité. De là naît, chez les dandys, cette attitude hautaine de caste provoquante, même dans sa froideur.

In this case his egotism and offended taste cause him to rebel against certain aspects of society. However, the ideal dandy simply asserts himself, unaware that his self-assertion is in fact a rebellion againt society and the cosmos. In the end, social protest is a theme because it is unavoidable. The dandy is a member of society despite himself. He is caught in a social context, and as a man of supremely good taste he does not long resist protesting against its bad taste. The difference between the ideal and actual dandy is one of direction, intent, awareness; and this distinction is all-important.

SUMMARY

Egotism motivates the rebel, but just as it is expressed in different forms, so there are in general three types of the rebel. First, he is a social rebel like Sorel, Antony, Rastignac, all three of whom are aware of the reason for and the fact of their rebellion. The exception, Hernani, acts as a blind egocentric force. Second, he is a metaphysical rebel like Vigny's Satan, who defies divine law, although there may be social repercussions as with Hans of Iceland. Third, the social and metaphysical aspects may fuse, as they do in the dandy. Moreover, all three types belong to the archetypal self-conscious hero. For unlike the herdman, who is a conformist, they all possess the awareness which causes their acute dissatisfaction with reality, and the romantic sensibility which inevitably motivates their rebellion against society or the cosmos.

SIX

THE ANTI-HERO

IT IS strange that one kind of romantic protagonist should be the anti-hero. Yet there he is—the epitome of weakness and the antithesis of the romantic hero. There is nothing grand or noble about his vacillation and weakness, as there is for example with Adolphe's. The anti-hero is often absurd, and nothing is more unheroic than an object of ridicule. He is indeed problematic in a study of the romantic hero.

The anti-hero is important for two reasons. First, he is by definition the other side of the coin—the antithesis of the romantic hero. He is the protagonist whose self-consciousness results in a critical, ironic, debilitating self-analysis. He is the hero of "what might have been," but who never in fact achieves heroic proportions. Second, he is much closer to the romantic hero than it may appear. The two figures merge in some ways. Ruy Blas is, for example, a romantic hero, yet at times he displays the most lamentable weakness. Since he is so painfully conscious of his low birth, even while disguised as a nobleman, he becomes pathetically weak whenever challenged by those who recognize him. At such times he cannot act; he can only comment laconically upon his weakness. Thus one fact is clear: In both cases, either when the anti-hero is antithetical to the romantic hero or when fused with him, self-consciousness is his motor force. This fact is a touchstone for understanding the anti-hero and his relationship to the romantic hero; it means that both protagonists, hero and anti-hero, are descended from the archetypal self-conscious hero. They simply express their awareness and romantic sensibility in different ways.

THE BACKGROUND

The anti-hero first appears as a theme in reaction to the romantic hero's emotional excesses. Musset writes in "La Coupe et les lèvres":[1]

> Mais je hais les pleurards, les rêveurs à nacelles,
> Les amants de la nuit, des lacs, des cascatelles,
> Cette engeance sans nom, qui ne peut faire un pas
> Sans s'inonder de vers, de pleurs et d'agendas.
> La nature, sans doute, est comme on veut la prendre.
> Il se peut, après tout, qu'ils sachent la comprendre;
> Mais eux, certainement, je ne les comprends pas.

It is a significant statement in the development of the anti-hero. Musset obviously believes that the hero wallows in emotion which he simulates more often than feels, and he attacks the man of sensibility for wearing his heart on his sleeve. Whether Musset is justified or not is unimportant beside his contention that the romantic hero is in fact not very heroic.

It is difficult to visualize the ideal man whom Musset would contrast with the romantic hero. He portrays a series of anti-heroes who are even more ineffectual by their detachment and neurasthenic self-appraisal than the romantic hero is by his extravagance and hypersensibility. Without formulating an ideal hero Musset implies that he should be much saner and more detached than the romantic hero.

Several other romantic writers agree. Gautier writes, for instance, that "mes vers/ Sont des vers de jeune homme et non un catéchisme."[2] In "Albertus" he assumes an air of flippancy which contrasts sharply with typical romantic high seriousness. He concludes the poem:[3]

> —J'aurais, pu clairement expliquer chaque chose,
> Clouer à chaque mot une savante glose.—
> Je vous crois, cher lecteur, assez spirituel
> Pour me comprendre.—Ainsi, bonsoir. Fermez la porte,
> Donnez-moi la pincette, et dites qu'on m'apporte
> Un tome de Pantagruel.

He makes a foppish dandy of the devil and humorously moves through Gothic bric-à-brac which many another romantic would use as the backdrop to grand passion. The recurrent motif is the hero's detachment, his ability to criticize himself and see himself objectively—to realize, in short, that he is ludicrous. In "Passereau l'écolier" from Borel's *Contes immoraux* the hero epitomizes such humorous detachment when he requests his executioner: "Je désirerais ardemment que vous me guillotinassiez."[4] Perhaps Mérimée uses restraint and detachment more than any other romantic writer. His heroes and heroines rarely feel grand romantic passions even during their most violent moments. Indeed, he carries detachment to such a point that in *Chronique du règne de Charles IX* he concludes the novel:[5]

Mergy se consola-t-il? Diane prit-elle un autre amant? Je le laisse à décider au lecteur, qui, de la sorte, terminera toujours le roman à son gré.

By intruding reality into fiction he breaks the illusion which underlies imaginative literature. His dénouement reveals a primary trait of the anti-hero—romantic irony. In tragic irony the reader is aware of the hero's real identity while the hero himself is not, but in romantic irony the reader is not certain who or what the hero really is because the hero himself is similarly confused. Mérimée does not often use romantic irony, but his detachment is a stage of development. It lays the background for the appearance of the anti-hero.

These writers believe that the hero should be more detached, and they implicitly or explicitly attack him for his extravagance. They attack him, moreover, in the most damning way; they ridicule him. They portray several anti-heroic types without formulating a concept of the ideal man. First, he is the supreme sophisticate whose actions are abortive because he is too sophisticated to take life very seriously. Second, he is the weakling who cannot act although he retains his hypersensitivity; he despises himself for his weakness. He would indeed be heroic in a different setting, but he feels he can do nothing in his own context. Third, there is a fusion of the hero and the anti-hero, as illustrated by Ruy Blas. These are the three fundamental types of the anti-hero.

THE SOPHISTICATE

In Musset's play *La Nuit Vénitienne* Razetta feels a grand passion for Laurette, and when she rejects him he exclaims effusively in the romantic tradition:[6]

Laurette! Laurette! Ah! je me sens plus lâche qu'une femme. Mon désespoir me tue: il faut que je pleure.

His despair amuses the sophisticated young Venetians. They wryly comment upon his love for Laurette; in contrast they enjoy casual liaisons while conscious that their love will pass. They are realistic, cynical, and regard him as a naive young fool. His dramatic foil is the supreme sophisticate, Prince Eysenach, whose wife, Laurette, is Razetta's former mistress. The Prince is unperturbed to learn that his wife has been unfaithful; he does not vent jealousy, anger, or hatred. After discovering that she intends to kill him, he merely discourses upon love and life, casually yet affectionately. He sees himself and her love-affair as part of a universal comedy. At length his sophistication conquers her, and she walks off with him after the assigned hour of murder, thus expressing her love for her husband and her rejection of Razetta. Then Razetta is confused. Should he scale the walls to kill Prince Eysenach or commit suicide in despair? At that moment the young Venetians again pass and goodnaturedly tease him for his naiveté:[7]

Veux-tu tuer ton rival, ou te noyer? Laisse ces idées communes au vulgaire des amants; souviens-toi de toi-même, et ne donne pas le mauvais exemple. Demain matin les femmes seront inabord-

ables, si on apprend cette nuit que Razetta s'est noyé. Encore
une fois, viens souper avec nous.

He renounces murder and suicide and accepts their offer;
and as he does he ceases to be a romantic hero. He rather
becomes a sophisticate, a man who laconically comments
upon himself until he in fact no longer feels the very emotions he ridicules.

In *On ne badine pas avec l'amour* the sophisticate, Perdican, falls in love with Camille, a romantic heroine. Their
relationship is doomed because they have different ideas on
love. She once asks:[8]

Lève la tête, Perdican! quel est l'homme qui ne croit à rien?

Perdican: En voilà un; je ne crois pas à la vie immortelle.
—Ma soeur chérie, les religieuses t'ont donné leur expérience;
mais, crois-moi, ce n'est pas la tienne; tu ne mourras pas sans
aimer.

As a sophisticate Perdican has enjoyed his share of mistresses.
He states frankly that he may not only have others after their
marriage, but also that he does not object to her taking a
lover if their love should die. And love, he adds, so frequently
dies. Camille is affronted and hurt, for she is religious and
believes that love should be an undying passion. He scoffs
at such a romantic view, though he is not unfeeling. He
displays his feeling and in the same breath justifies his idea
by arguing:[9]

Adieu, Camille, retourne à ton couvent, et lorsqu'on te fera de
ces récits hideux qui t'ont empoisonnée, réponds ce que je vais
te dire: Tous les hommes sont menteurs, inconstants, faux,
bavards, hypocrites, orgueilleux ou lâches, méprisables et sen-
suels; toutes les femmes sont perfides, artificielles, vaniteuses,
curieuses et dépravées; mais il y a au monde une chose sainte et
sublime, c'est l'union de deux de ces êtres si imparfaits et si
affreux. On est souvent trompé en amour, souvent blessé et
souvent malheureux; mais on aime, et, quand on est sur le bord
de sa tombe, on se retourne pour regarder en arrière, et on se
dit: J'ai souffert souvent, je me suis trompé quelquefois, mais

j'ai aimé. C'est moi qui ai vécu, et non pas un être factice créé par mon orgueil et mon ennui.

His cynicism contrasts with what a romantic hero would typically say. They never consummate their love, and their ultimate separation is of course inevitable. As a sophisticate Perdican can neither understand nor sympathize with the romantic Camille.

THE WEAKLING

The anti-hero is a weakling who possesses a certain potentiality which he never realizes. In *Les Caprices de Marianne* Célio and Octave are both such weaklings. Unable to express his love to Marianne, Claudio's wife, Célio asks his best friend, Octave, to serve as his go-between, since Octave has access, as a relative, to Claudio's home. Marianne scoffs at Célio's passion but in time falls in love with Octave; she intimates she wants him as her lover. His suspicions aroused, Claudio is incensed and plots Célio's death. And believing that Octave has betrayed him with Marianne, Célio calmly commits suicide by walking into Claudio's trap.

Célio and Octave are clearly men of deep feeling. They possess the hero's sensibility, but they do not evidence his heroism or titanism. Their actions are abortive, never heroic or titanic. Octave falls in love with Marianne while pleading for Célio, who does not have enough courage to speak for himself. He is not a romantic man of action who would scale a castle wall to flee with her in the night. He simply cannot act. But unlike Adolphe his inability to act does not result from abulia or vacillation, but rather from the failure of his will to equal his desire, from the failure of his will even to struggle with desire. The anti-hero comes on stage defeated. A romantic hero like Adolphe expresses his emotions inwardly even when he cannot express them outwardly, whereas an anti-hero like Célio is not even torn apart emotionally. The element of titanic struggle is missing.

There is a whimpering quality in their weakness. Célio describes the hopelessness of his love:[10]

Pourquoi donc suis-je ainsi? pourquoi ne saurais-je aimer cette femme comme toi, Octave, tu l'aimerais, ou comme j'en aimerais une autre? Qui pourrait dire?

This simpering aspect is reflected as Octave learns of his best friend Célio's death. Rather than taking immediate revenge, as a romantic hero would, he mutters:[11]

Célio m'aurait vengé, si j'étais mort pour lui comme il est mort pour moi. Son tombeau m'appartient; c'est moi qu'ils ont étendu dans cette sombre allée; c'est pour moi qu'ils avaient aiguisé leurs épées; c'est pour moi qu'ils ont tué!

And he correctly adds: "Je ne suis qu'un débauché sans coeur."[12] Even the romantic hero's weakness is titanic, i.e., bigger than life, but the anti-hero's weakness is whimpering, petty.

André del Sarto, in the play of the same name, is Musset's completest portrayal of weakness. The great painter steals King Francis's money at his faithless wife's insistence, and then he runs away to Italy. Lucrèce repays him with cuckoldom. Del Sarto exclaims:[13]

Que faisait-elle de mal en me demandant ce qui lui plaisait? Et moi, je lui donnais parce qu'elle me le demandait, rien de plus; faiblesse maudite! pas une réflexion! . . . à quoi tient donc l'honneur?

His weakness is doubly tragic because he is undeniably a genius and yet fawns before his wife:[14]

Les instants que nous passons ensemble sont si courts et si rares! et ils me sont si chers! . . . Vous seule au monde, Lucrèce, me consolez du chagrin qui m'obsède. . . . Ah! si je vous perdais! . . . tout mon courage, toute ma philosophie est dans vos yeux.

She does not love him; she even mocks him for his spinelessness. And when she finally deserts him for her lover, Del Sarto commits suicide in despair. Yet love is still on his lips as he dies:[15]

C'est un cordial puissant. Approche-le de tes lèvres, et tu seras guéri, quel que soit le mal dont tu souffres. Vos mains, et adieu, chers amis. . . . Oh, combien je l'aimais!

Even in death he realizes that his love is a sign of weakness. He is a tragic figure because such strength coexists with such weakness—all the strength of creative genius, all the weakness of an anti-hero.

THE ARCHETYPE

But if the anti-hero is defined as a protagonist who is antipodal to the romantic hero in every respect, then obviously Célio and Del Sarto are not pure examples. Célio possesses some potentiality, and Del Sarto is a great painter. In spite of their weakness both men evidence a certain potentiality for heroism; they simply do not express it. It is otherwise with Musset's Fantasio, who lacks every trace of heroism as a protagonist. Since he is most clearly the romantic hero's antithesis, Fantasio may be considered the archetypal anti-hero.

Although published in 1834 during the height of French romanticism, *Fantasio* is foreign to the romantic spirit. Fantasio is in fact no hero at all. He is neither a poet-prophet guiding the people, nor a Promethean rebel evoking the wrath of the gods, nor a wanderer engaged on the romantic quest, nor a man of romantic sensibility. He is not pathological. In short, he evinces none of the romantic hero's titanism.

Fantasio is an intelligent, hypersensitive scoundrel. Although he acts apart from the herd, he does not tower above them. His friendship with Spark, Hartmann, and Facio shows that he has an earthy sense of camaraderie for his fellows. He is not a romantic solitary brooding apart in grand isolation. The romantic hero sometimes substitutes emotion for mind, but Fantasio dulls his hypersensitivity by drinking. "Il faut que je me grise,"[16] he says, and he feels that a display of emotion is emotionalism.

Although he is not heroic, Fantasio yet differs markedly from the herdman. He has greater emotional sensitivity, and he falls prey to despair and cynicism in his attempt to be realistic. He speaks nostalgically of his penchant for art when he was a boy, and he makes a quip the next moment. He distrusts himself and does not want to be the victim of his rationalizations. He is indeed an acute observer with much insight into life. He notes, for instance, in the romantic tradition:[17]

Hélas! tout ce que les hommes se disent entre eux se ressemble; les idées qu'ils échangent sont presque toujours les mêmes dans toutes leurs conversations; mais, dans l'intérieur de toutes ces machines isolées, quels replis, quels compartiments secrets! C'est tout un monde que chacun porte en lui! un monde ignoré qui naît et qui meurt en silence!

His deep frustration is evident. He obviously suffers, yet quips in the same breath that his only real concern is to continue to elude his creditors. And once more he turns to wine.

Fantasio knows he is a scamp, but occasionally he yearns for what might have been. His actions are antithetical to the hero's. He is whimsical and his struggle to evade his creditors farcical. There is no romantic fire in him, and indeed he refers to himself as a "vièille cheminée sans feu."[18] The image contrasts sharply with the volcanic romantic hero.

Consider for example the romantic motif of flight. Fantasio dresses in the dead jester Saint-Jean's clothes in order to hide in the King's court from his creditors. He does not commit a crime, defy them, or even disdain to recognize that he in fact owes something to the herd. His action is antithetical to the romantic motif of flight to the wilderness, the Alps, the lonely places where the soul communes with itself; there is no passion or violence. Moreover, his assumption of the fool's garb represents a certain compromise with the world. He fails to preserve his integrity, whereas the archetypal romantic hero adamantly refuses all compromise. By becoming a court-fool Fantasio symbolically discards the last thread of his integrity.

His action is nonetheless reasonable if one grants his stated

assumption that man is by nature a ludicrous ass. He exclaims:[19]

Quelle misérable chose que l'homme! ne pas pouvoir seulement
sauter par sa fenêtre sans se casser les jambes! être obligé de
jouer du violon dix ans pour devenir un musicien passable!
Apprendre pour être peintre, pour être palefrenier! Apprendre
pour faire une omelette!

Man is helpless but whereas the romantic hero says that man
can be grand in his helplessness, Fantasio says that he is
merely ludicrous. No superman thunders from the peak; no
inexplicable passion impels him on strange quests to exotic
lands. Fantasio's observation about man contrasts with the
poet-prophet's belief that he perceives reality suprration-
ally. Fantasio would rather quip that man, especially the
poet-prophet, must study to become a good ostler. Romantic
genius, cardinal in any idea of the romantic hero, is not at
all present.

As an anti-hero Fantasio displays sensitivity but not passion
or even strong emotion. Unlike Ruy Blas he does not love
a princess; he is not a worm enamored of a star. He pointedly
observes:[20]

L'amour n'existe plus, mon cher ami. La religion, sa nourrice, a
les mamelles pendantes comme une vieille bourse au fond de
laquelle il y a un gros sou.

He does not try to usurp the Prince's place in Elsbeth's affection. And just as there is no love, so there are no other great
passions. There is only his longing for wine, which brings
nepenthe—sweet forgetfulness.

This depiction of Fantasio's character is meaningful. If
he had so wished, Musset could have developed a plot
in which Fantasio, dressed as a fool, enters the King's court,
woos the beautiful Princess, and kills the cruel, foppish
Prince of Mantoue. Moreover, such a plot would be in the
grand romantic tradition. Yet Musset does not do this. He
sketches Fantasio as an anti-hero in his reaction to romantic
excesses. Thus Fantasio continues to pun cynically:[21]

Un calembour console de bien des chagrins; et jouer avec les mots est un moyen comme un autre de jouer avec les pensées, les actions et les êtres. Tout est calembour ici-bas, et il est aussi difficile de comprendre le regard d'un enfant de quatre ans, que le galimatias de trois drames modernes.

He feels no desire to change his life or apologize for his actions. Life is absurd.

Another example is instructive. The romantic hero often perpetrates, or feels he perpetrates, enormous crimes, but Fantasio's crime is no more than a caprice. He snatches the Prince's wig from his head. The page humorously recounts the incident to Princess Elsbeth:[22]

La perruque s'est enlevée en l'air au bout d'un hameçon. Nous l'avons retrouvée dans l'office, à côté d'une bouteille cassée; on ignore qui a fait cette plaisanterie. Mais le duc n'est pas moins furieux, et il a juré que, si l'auteur n'en est pas puni de mort, il déclarera la guerre au roi votre père, et mettra tout à feu et à sang.

The entire episode is an absurd contrast with the romantic hero's grand passion. Musset underscores this basic absurdity by having the Prince demand the death-penalty while the King finds the crime heinous enough only for a stiff prison-sentence.

There is no room for the romantic hero in such a ludicrous universe. Hence the protagonist emerges as a man no less absurd than life itself, and Fantasio comments while in prison: "En vérité, lorsque je suis gris, je crois que j'ai quelque chose de surhumain."[23] He means that when he is drunk he has a clearer perception of the world than at any other time. Then he sees how ridiculous men really are, and he is superior because he is always drunk.

The court, like life itself, is ludicrous because the reader rejects in the satire the values which the characters themselves accept. To be sure, Fantasio is not quite part of his world nor entirely separated from it. He is not a romantic rebel, yet rebelliousness though attenuated and abortive is undeniably a motive. And when Elsbeth offers him a position as court-jester, he replies:[24]

Je le voudrais de grand coeur; mais, en vérité, si j'y étais forcé, je sauterais par la fenêtre pour me sauver un de ces jours.

The persona of whimsicality cracks, and the reader perceives the anti-heroic character. Fantasio reveals himself as what he might have been—if the structure of society were different, if he were of a different rank, if only so many factors could be changed. Then, perhaps, he would become a romantic hero who could express the latent passions which he must now dull through wine and irony. Yet the reader is not quite sure. Indeed, romantic irony results from the reader's ultimate uncertainty about Fantasio's real identity. Just as Fantasio does not know himself, so the reader never comes to know him. Consequently the play is a masterful study in romantic irony, and as the hero of what might have been, Fantasio is the supreme example of the anti-hero.

THE FUSION

As a fusion of the romantic hero and anti-hero Ruy Blas is admittedly more the former than the latter. He is nonetheless instructive in a study of the anti-hero because he represents the fusion of heroic and unheroic elements as much as any other romantic character. Hugo characteristically sets the scene by antithesis when writing that Ruy Blas is a valet with a nobleman's soul, whereas his master is a nobleman with a valet's soul. The play depicts what one very noble, talented valet named Ruy Blas does, as a romantic hero, once he has the opportunity. In this way Hugo emphasizes the importance of the social context, and he implies clearly that the anti-hero cannot become a hero without an opportunity, regardless of his potentiality. Otherwise society stifles him.

Heroic passions lie dormant in Ruy Blas and merely await the moment for self-expression. He characterizes himself:[25]

J'avais je ne sais quelle ambition au coeur.
Je marchais, je croyais tout réel, tout possible,

J'espérais tout du sort!—Et puis je suis de ceux
Qui passent tout un jour, pensifs et paresseux,
Devant quelque palais regorgeant de richesses,
A regarder entrer et sortir des duchesses.—
Si bien qu'un jour, mourant de faim sur le pavé,
J'ai ramassé du pain, frère, où j'en ai trouvé;
Dans la fainéantise et dans l'ignominie.
Oh! quand j'avais vingt ans, crédule à mon génie,
Je me perdais, marchant pieds nus dans les chemins,
En méditations sur le sort des humains;
J'avais bâti des plans sur tout,—une montagne
De projets.—Je plaignais le malheur de l'Espagne.
Ami, le résultat, tu le vois.—Un laquais!

He shows his ability as a man of action whenever he has the opportunity. He reveals his love for the Queen and becomes in fact the nobleman of his dreams. Yet when Don Salluste confronts him with his deception, Ruy Blas breaks down:[26]

Oh! vous êtes un homme effrayant. Mes genoux
Tremblent. . . Vous m'entraînez vers un gouffre invisible.
Oh! je sens que je suis dans une main terrible!
Vous avez des projets monstrueux. J'entrevoi
Quelque chose d'horrible. . . . —Ayez pitié de moi!
Il faut que je vous dise,—hélas! jugez vous-même!
Vous ne le saviez pas! cette femme, je l'aime.

His impotence is overwhelming; in a moment he changes from a hero to a weakling. He is in character only if it is remembered that his antipodal roles as romantic hero and anti-hero struggle with each other, first one gaining ascendancy, then the other. When he is with Don Salluste, Ruy Blas is the anti-hero, the man of potentiality whose faculties are paralyzed by his low social station. A pillar of strength as the romantic hero, he thus becomes a weakling as the anti-hero:[27]

Je suis fou. Je n'ai plus une idée en son lieu.
Ma raison, dont j'étais si vain, mon Dieu! mon Dieu!
Prise en un tourbillon d'épouvante et de rage.

N'est plus qu'un pauvre jonc tordu par un orage!—
Such is the tragedy of the fused hero.

SUMMARY

The romantic hero and the anti-hero are both motivated by self-consciousness, i.e., awareness plus the romantic sensibility, though they evince far different traits. The anti-hero, too, is self-conscious and does possess heroic potentiality. He is aware of the forces which mold him and the social forces against which he struggles. But self-consciousness is differently oriented in the anti-hero, since it represents his ironic appraisal of self in the social context.

All anti-heroes evidence romantic irony to some extent, and this theme becomes even more important in post-romantic works like Flaubert's *l'Education sentimentale.* The anti-hero, like the poet-prophet, is moving away from the romantic spirit into something else, as the visionary moves into symbolism. However, the anti-hero still remains in the romantic tradition even while struggling in and against the forces of the tradition. He emerges most clearly in Musset's plays. Whether as a sophisticate or weakling, or as a fusion with the romantic hero, the anti-hero always observes himself and he wryly comments upon his own weakness. He withers under his own debilitating irony, turned within.

CONCLUSION

WE NOW have a map of the romantic terrain, and it is time to see what lands we have traversed and what remains yet unexplored.

The critic who tries to understand the romantic hero takes a certain risk, for he must first formulate a theoretical basis for the hero. And in probing why, in assessing points of similarity and difference, in studying both the general background and actual manifestation of romanticism, the critic may over-intellectualize and fail to communicate the fire and sense of urgency present even in bad romantic writing. This is unfortunate. But this study is obviously, and perhaps regrettably, not concerned with esthetic evaluation.

It is rather an attempt to define the romantic hero and trace his principal lines of development. It is a rather philosophical study concerned with principles, and a full descriptive treatment of all the romantic heroes awaits a definitive history. Yet this study can offer a new approach to romanticism, the complex and often unappreciated movement which has fathered contemporary literature: It strikes at the heart of romanticism through the romantic hero. It assumes that the hero is the key to understanding romanticism, that he reflects the values which characterize him and motivate him.

It fills a historical gap since there has not previously been a real analytic study of the romantic hero. Earlier work—and it is surprisingly scanty—has been descriptive and evaluative, not analytic and interpretative.

What can we be certain about?

Our definition of the romantic hero rests upon two fundamental assumptions. First, romanticism is a movement which emphasizes imagination, sensibility, and the will, and which reinterprets reason. Second, the hero is the self-conscious protagonist of the literature which reflects these semantic changes in imagination, sensibility, will, reason. These two assumptions have been verified by examining romantic documents. Self-consciousness is the common denominator of the romantic hero as he is cast in his different roles. He essentially belongs to one hero-type rather than to a series of heroes. He merely reveals himself differently while still remaining in each instance the self-conscious hero. Indeed, the self-conscious hero is the archetypal hero whose two distinguishing traits, acute awareness and romantic sensibility, characterize each different kind of the romantic hero.

The archetypal self-conscious hero becomes a particular variety of romantic hero by responding differently with his romantic sensibility to his awareness. His response follows certain definite patterns. In this connection he generally assumes one of five roles or a pseudo-role. He is a seeker, a man of fate, a pathological hero, a poet-prophet, or a rebel. In his pseudo-role he is the anti-hero, i.e., the man who comments ironically upon his weakness though he is potentially heroic. These are the principal lines of descent from the archetype.

At least two of the roles are like those of earlier hero-types. Certainly every literary protagonist is a seeker who is looking for something in life, and every hero is to a certain extent a man of fate since he is a creature of a social and/or cosmic context. This is not to say that the romantic seeker and man of fate are, by any means, linear descendants of previous heroes. The difference between the romantic hero and earlier hero-types is more accentuated in the case of the pathological hero, for no other types evidence his peculiar patterns of hypersensibility. He differs most from earlier types as a poet-prophet or rebel. Yet whatever the degree of his resemblance to earlier heroes, there are nonetheless basic points of striking difference.

The romantic hero is a seeker. He is actively engaged on a quest, the romantic direction of which makes him a hero. His most salient trait is superiority, whether real or fancied. Since he is superior his aims and motives differ from the herdman's, and he both misunderstands and is misunderstood. In this role he may move through society as a figure of grand isolation—the solitary. Or since he is indeed superior, he may feel responsible for the herd, which is lost without him. In this event he becomes the leader of his people, and his self-conscious superiority leads him to forge a bond with the herdman.

Every seeker engages on the quest in one of three ways. He is a wanderer, thinker, or mystic. The object of the goal varies in each case though it is always subsumed by the romantic dichotomy reality-ideality.

René is, for instance, a wanderer who turns to the New World in his search for ideality, i.e., an ideal state of reality. Obermann, as a wanderer, externalizes his search of ideality through actual trips. The fact that at best they only partially realize their quest is secondary to the fact of their search. The actual voyage is of course a spiritual voyage.

Yet it is not necessary for the seeker to be a wanderer. Like Vigny he may be a thinker who equates ideality with knowledge, spiritual certainty. He approaches ideality, i.e., the ideal state of reality, through science in a rational if hostile world. The voyage-motif is secondary, since the seeker is fundamentally a thinker.

The seeker is also a mystic who knows intuitively, suprarationally. Knowledge is, as in Hugo's "Ce que dit la bouche d'ombre," divine illumination or a glimpse into the essence of reality, i.e., ideality. Nerval, for example, understands the immutable verities of life by stripping away cultural contingencies and glimpsing the essence of truth itself. The seeker as mystic is suprarational because rationalism is indeed an ineffective mode of understanding.

The romantic hero is a man of fate. There are two aspects to his role, fated and fatal, and indeed he may be both at once. He is fated, like Antony, whenever his end is fore-ordained as the effect of certain causes in a given context, and he is fatal, like Bug-Jargal, whenever he destroys others as the cause of certain adverse effects. Necessity is the prime factor—an elaboration of the fact that cause results in effect. It is Calvinistic in intensity, as with Vigny. Fatality is conceived in both social and cosmic contexts, and the man of fate is either fated, fatal, or both at once, caught in the web of his weaving. Yet he is radically different from earlier tragic heroes as a result of his self-consciousness, which focuses him in a post-classic light and leads him in a new romantic direction.

The romantic hero is a pathological hero, though it is sometimes difficult to ascertain where hypersensibility ends and pathology begins. One fact is always certain. The hero, as a superior man, has greater energy than the herdman and thus a wider emotional range. His patterns of sensibility are not the herdman's. In short, he is by definition a man of hypersensibility since he is a hero. Whenever his responses are exaggerated enough, then he becomes a pathological hero. There are two broad categories. The man of hypersensibility turns either inward in self-analysis or outward in action; he is passive like Adolphe or active like Sorel, or he may be a fusion like René. Activity and passivity are the categories of hypersensibility, but they are not always found in a pristine form.

The matter is subtle since there is a great variation in emotional intensity. But certainly the pathological hero grows from the man of hypersensibility, and pathological responses are often glaringly evident. For instance, Adolphe suffers from abulia, Octave from neurasthenia, René is a manic-depressive type. Algolagnia, obsessive guilt, sexual perversion are recurrent themes in Baudelaire's *Les Fleurs du*

Praz's *Romantic Agony,* moreover, is a long *catalogue*
iné of the various pathological themes in romanticism.
rsensibility may be so intense and exaggerated that the
like the schizophrenic Nerval, goes mad. Self-conscious-
can be heightened disastrously, for at least in this case
eness and the romantic sensibility react like chemical
ts and explode in the form of the pathological hero.

he romantic hero is the poet-prophet. It is he who knows
Word as a solitary, leader of his people, or visionary, and
who brings the Word to his people. As a magus and a solitary he may direct mankind from afar. In this role he is generally a prototype of Moses, as a leader, pointing the way to
the Promised Land across the wilderness. His priestly function as a visionary is to perceive the infinite and the absolute,
and then he records his mystical experience in a poetic form
which enables the reader to relive his own experience. Sometimes, indeed, he becomes so preoccupied with the Message
that he tends to forget his audience, the herd. In all three
cases the poet-prophet is descended from the ancient *vates,*
seer, the divinely inspired orphic poet afflicted with sacred
madness, the mouthpiece of the gods. He knows the Word
by revelation.

The poet-prophet responds to his role in several ways. He
may be an isolated, unhappy leader of the herd, like Vigny's
Moïse, or a leader like Hugo's magus in "La Fonctioh du
poète" and "Les Mages." The poet-prophet may also feel
that society rejects him, like Stello, Chatterton, Baudelaire;
or again like Hugo he is convinced that he is indissolubly
linked with his people. On the other hand, Nerval is undis-
turbed by his social isolation, since he is rather concerned
with his poetic visions, i.e., with the Message itself.

The romantic hero is a rebel. There are, moreover, three
aspects to his rebellion—social, metaphysical, and a fusion.
He may deliberately assail society, oppose God or the cosmos,
or do both at once. Hernani is an exception since he is primarily an egocentric force whose revolt is self-assertion rather

than a conscious assault against an established moral or social order.

Julien Sorel and Eugène de Rastignac manipulate the precepts of society to their advantage as social rebels. Hugo, Lamartine, Vigny, and Baudelaire are metaphysical rebels with their satanism when they assert a new religious code or reinterpret the traditional code in a new way. The rebel may also be a seeker who unlocks the forbidden secrets of the universe. He may, like Hans of Iceland, incarnate nihilism and oppose the life-principle itself. As a fusion of the social and metaphysical rebel, the dandy is a special case. In theory he does not have an adversary, but in actuality most French dandies do assault society, God, the moral code. It is virtually impossible for them to do otherwise, for they cannot live and act in a vacuum.

The dandy's self-consciousness results in egocentrism, egomania, both of which provide the motor force causing him to assert himself, and this self-assertion, rebellious by definition, often leads to criminality. Many of Barbey's dandies, for example, become criminals, just as Hernani, a prime example of the rebel, is an outlaw. Like the hero in his other roles, the rebel is not usually a separate category. He most often fuses with the seeker, man of fate, pathological hero, poet-prophet. Here as elsewhere the romantic hero appears in many guises, and it is theoretically possible for him to be all five types at once. René, for instance, can be understood in every role except the poet-prophet.

The anti-hero is a separate category. He is the romantic protagonist whose self-consciousness results in a paralyzing self-criticism—a man who might have been heroic in a different setting. Artistic detachment, for instance in Mérimée, provides the background for his development. To be sure, the anti-hero sometimes fuses with the romantic hero, as he does in *Ruy Blas*. But usually he is the weakling or the supreme sophisticate.

It is Musset who is primarily interested in the anti-hero. In his drama he presents a series of anti-heroes, among whom Fantasio is archetypal since he best exemplifies the romantic irony which underlies a concept of the anti-hero. In tragic irony the reader has knowledge which the hero does not have, but in romantic irony the mask deluding the anti-hero also confuses the reader. Just as the anti-hero does not know himself, so the reader is never sure of his real identity. One fact is certain. Self-consciousness destroys Fantasio, as indeed all anti-heroes, since it makes him aware of his weakness without enabling him to focus and utilize his hypersensitivity.

What can we be certain about?

We know the romantic hero is the self-conscious hero, and romanticism is a self-conscious movement. It is the product of the greatest social cataclysm of modern history—the Revolution, industrialization, scientific and technological progress, philosophical and ethical reorientation, the disintegration of hierarchy. Romantic literature reflects this era of violent social change; it captures the spirit of the age in its literary hero. And the hero's problems are the concern of his age. Surely this, if anything, is certain: The thinking man during the romantic movement posited several questions which he desperately sought to answer.

If the old values are invalid, what can man believe? He must engage on a quest to resolve the old problem, conceived in different terms, of reality-ideality.

Is man's place in the universe mechanistically determined? The romantic's interest in the man of fate is not coincidental.

Can anything be really known about man except quantitatively, so that normalcy and pathology are a matter of statistics? The hypersensibility-pathological hero problem shows how the romantics ponder the intricacies of this question.

What can the poet's place be in a society which denies him one? The poet-prophet reflects their deep concern, their burning desire to fill again a role which was perhaps lost forever in the social cataclysm.

Finally, are the traditional codes contingent or absolute? Are they really meaningful? Can a new social or moral code replace them? Are they worth preservation? What is, in fact, the good, the true, the beautiful? The romantic rebel emerges from this atmosphere, accepting nothing, questioning everything, asserting himself as a law when there is no law.

So it is only natural that this self-conscious age, which questions the traditional values and formulates the new, should find its ultimate literary expression in the self-conscious hero—the romantic hero.

NOTES

INTRODUCTION

1. Quoted in Francisque Vial and Louis Denise, *Idées et doctrines littéraires du XIX siècle* (Paris: Delagrave, 1928), pp. 87-88.
2. See Jacques Barzun, *Romanticism and the Modern Ego* (Boston: Little, Brown, 1944), p. 138.
3. Cf. Arthur O. Lovejoy, "On the Discrimination of Romanticisms," *PMLA*, XXXIX (1924), 229-53; Joseph Aynard, "Comment définir le romantisme?", *Revue de littérature comparée*, V (1925), 641-58; and see also J. G. Robertson, *Studies in the Genesis of Romantic Theory in the Eighteenth Century* (Cambridge, England: Cambridge University Press, 1923), pp. 290-91.
4. Barzun, p. 20.
5. Robertson, *loc. cit.*
6. Emile Deschamps, *La Préface des études françaises et étrangères*, ed. Henri Girard (Paris: Presses françaises, 1923), p. xxix.
7. *Ibid.*, p. 6.
8. Barzun, p. 58.
9. William J. Handy, *Poetry as Knowledge: The Kantian Tradition in Modern Literary Theory* (unpub. diss., U. of Oklahoma, 1954), pp. 35-37.
10. Barzun, pp. 78-79.
11. See Basil Willey, *The Seventeenth Century Background* (Garden City: Doubleday, 1955), p. 287; and Paul Hazard, *La Crise de la conscience européenne* (Paris: Boivin, 1935), pp. 355-56.
12. Cf. Albert Joseph George, *The Development of French Romanticism* (Syracuse: Syracuse University Press, 1955), p. 190.
13. Louis Maigron, *Le Romantisme et les moeurs* (Paris: Champion, 1910), p. 7.
14. N. H. Clement, *Romanticism in France* (New York: MLA, 1939), p. 1.
15. Barzun, p. 193.
16. Clement, pp. 445-46.
17. Walter Jackson Bate, *From Classic to Romantic* (Cambridge, Mass.: Harvard University Press, 1946), p. 11.

CHAPTER ONE

1. Francois-Auguste de Chateaubriand, *René* (Paris: Droz, 1935), p. 32.
2. *Ibid.*, pp. 30-31.
3. *Ibid.*, p. 27. Cf. Sainte-Beuve's observation, *Chateaubriand et son groupe littéraire sous l'empire* (Paris: Calmann Lévy, 1889), I, p. 101: "Pareil aux fleuves *descendant du sein de Jupiter*, le voilà donc à sa source cet ennui qui va s'épancher à travers le monde, qui cherchera partout l'infini et l'indéterminè, le *désert*. . . ."
4. *Ibid.*, p. 46.
5. *Ibid.*, p. 33.
6. François-Auguste de Chateaubriand, *Les Natchez* (Paris: Droz, 1932), p. 222.
7. *Ibid.*, p. 367.
8. François-Auguste de Chateaubriand, *Le Génie du christianisme*, in *Oeuvres complètes* (Paris: Garnier, n.d.), II, p. 218. See especially Chapter IX, "Vague des passions," which the episode *René* illustrates.
9. Chateaubriand, *Les Natchez*, pp. 435-36.
10. François-Auguste de Chateaubriand, *Mémoires d'outre-tombe* (Paris: Garnier, 1930), I, pp. 154-55.
11. *Ibid.*, pp. xlvi-xlvii.
12. *Ibid.*, VI, p. 475.
13. *Ibid.*, I, pp. 312-13.
14. Albert Béguin, *L'Ame romantique et le rêve* (Paris: Corti, 1946), p. 332.
15. Sénancour, *Obermann* (Paris: Droz, 1931), I, p. 149.
16. *Ibid.*, I, p. 31.
17. *Ibid.*, II, p. 245.
18. Sénancour, *Rêveries sur la nature primitive de l'homme* (Paris: Droz, 1940), II, p. 178.
19. Sénancour, *Obermann*, I, p. 163.
20. *Ibid.*, I. p. 149.
21. Pierre-Georges Castex, *Vigny:*

l'homme et l'oeuvre (Paris: Boivin, 1952), p. 99.
22. Alfred de Vigny, *Servitude et grandeur militaires* (Paris: Conard, 1914), pp. 250-51.
23. Emile Faguet, *Dix-neuvième siècle* (Paris: Société française d'imprimerie et de librairie, n.d.), p. 128.
24. Gérard de Nerval, *Les Chimères*, ed. Jeanine Moulin (Genève: Droz, 1949), p. xxix.
25. *Ibid.*, p. xxxix.
26. *Ibid.*, p. 44.
27. Gérard de Nerval, *Octavie*, in *Oeuvres*, eds. Albert Béguin and Jean Richer (Paris: Gallimard, 1952), I, p. 363.
28. *Ibid.*, pp. 307-08.
29. Charles Baudelaire, *Les Fleurs du mal*, eds. Jacques Crépet and Georges Blin (Paris: Corti, 1950), p. 160.
30. *Ibid.*, p. 161.
31. *Ibid.*, p. 164.
32. *Ibid.*, p. 18.
33. *Ibid.*, pp. 57-58.
34. *Ibid.*, p. 165.

CHAPTER TWO

1. Edmond Estève, *Byron et le romantisme français* (Paris: Boivin, n.d.), p. 477.
2. Charles Baudelaire, *Les Fleurs du mal*, eds. Jacques Crépet and Georges Blin (Paris: Corti, 1950), p. 6.
3. Benjamin Constant, *Adolphe* (Paris: Droz, 1946), p. 15.
4. Benjamin Constant, *Cécile* (Paris: Gallimard, 1951), p. 85.
5. Alexandre Dumas *père*, *Antony*, in *Théâtre romantique* (Paris: Firmin-Didot, n.d.), pp. 149-50.
6. *Ibid.*, pp. 147-48.
7. *Ibid.*, p. 152.
8. *Ibid.*, p. 213.
9. François-Auguste de Chateaubriand, *René* (Paris: Droz, 1935), pp. 48-49.

10. François-Auguste de Chateaubriand, *Les Natchez* (Paris: Droz, 1932), pp. 330-31.
11. *Ibid.*, p. 367.
12. *Ibid.*, p. 331.
13. *Ibid.*, p. 435.
14. *Ibid.*, pp. 502-03.
15. Victor Hugo, *Hernani*, in *Théâtre II, Oeuvres complètes* (Paris: Ollendorff, 1926), p. 76.
16. *Ibid.*, p. 153.
17. Victor Hugo, *Bug-Jargal* (Paris: Ollendorff, n.d.), pp. 222-23.
18. Alfred de Vigny, *Les Destinées*, ed. Verdun L. Saulnier (Paris: Droz, 1947), p. xxxvi.
19. *Ibid.*, p. 12.
20. *Ibid.*, p. 16.
21. Alfred de Vigny, *Poëmes* (Paris: Conard, 1914), p. 15.
22. *Ibid.*, p. 27.
23. *Ibid.*, p. 39.
24. Adapted from Saulnier, *ibid.*, p. xl.
25. Cf. *ibid.*, pp. xxvii-xxxix.
26. Honoré de Balzac, *Peau de chagrin*, in *Oeuvres complètes* (Paris: Conard, 1925), p. 37.
27. *Ibid.*, p. 38.
28. Mario Praz, *The Romantic Agony* (London: Oxford University Press, 1951), p. 59.

CHAPTER THREE

1. François-Auguste de Chateaubriand, *René* (Paris: Droz, 1935), p. 77.
2. François-Auguste de Chateaubriand, *Atala* (Paris: Flammarion, n.d.), p. 87.
3. François-Auguste de Chateaubriand, *Les Natchez* (Paris: Droz, 1932), p. 335.
4. Benjamin Constant, *Adolphe* (Paris, Droz, 1946), p. 13.
5. Sénancour, *Obermann* (Paris: Droz, 1931), I, p. 24.
6. *Ibid.*, p. 98.
7. Henri-Marie Beyle, *Le Rouge et le noir* (Paris: Crès, 1922), p. 27.

I refer to my personal copy, though the definitive edition is Martineau's (Paris, Garnier, 1939).
8. *Ibid.*, p. 30.
9. *Ibid.*, p. 47.
10. *Ibid.*, p. 166.
11. *Ibid.*, p. 107.
12. *Ibid.*, p. 103.
13. Jules Barbey d'Aurevilly, *Du Dandysme et de Georges Brummell* (Paris: Emile-Paul, 1918), pp. vi-vii.
14. *Ibid.*, pp. 12-13.
15. Jean Canu, *Barbey d'Aurevilly* (Paris: Laffont, 1945), p. 491.
16. Jules Barbey d'Aurevilly, *op. cit.*, p. 13.
17. Elizabeth Creed, *Le Dandysme de Jules Barbey d'Aurevilly* (Paris: Droz, 1938), p. 4.
18. Canu, p. 89.
19. *Les Diaboliques* was first published in 1874, long after the formal close of the romantic movement, but I have included the book since it is indisputably in the romantic tradition and so well illustrates certain points. It is a mistake to be bound rigorously by artificial literary dates. After all, the greatest French romantic poetry was written by Hugo during his last period, a quarter of a century after the failure of *Les Burgraves*. I feel no need to apologize for including *Les Diaboliques*, though an explanation of my reason for doing so is of course in order.
20. Canu, pp. 91-92.
21. Constant, p. 7.
22. *Ibid.*, p. 50.
23. Sénancour, p. 27.
24. Beyle, p. 548.
25. Gérard de Nerval, *Aurélia*, in *Oeuvres* (Paris: Gallimard, 1952), I, p. 381.
26. Gérard de Nerval, *Les Chimères*, ed. Jeanine Moulin (Genève: Droz, 1949), p. xxxix.

27. Constant, p. 84.
28. *Ibid.*, p. 8.
29. Sénancour, p. 175.
30. Chateaubriand, *René*, p. 15.
31. Alfred de Musset, *La Confession d'un enfant du siècle*, in *Oeuvres complètes* (Paris: Garnier, n.d.), VII, p. 31.
32. *Ibid.*, pp. 250-51.
33. Sénancour, pp. 134-35.
34. *Ibid.*, p. 63.
35. Emile Faguet, *Dix-neuvième siècle* (Paris: Société française d'imprimerie et de librairie, n.d.), p. 140.
36. *Ibid.*
37. Charles Baudelaire, *Les Fleurs du mal*, eds. Jacques Crépet and Georges Blin (Paris: Corti, 1950), p. 85.
38. *Ibid.*, p. 172
39. Musset, p. 332.
40. Baudelaire, p. 15.
41. *Ibid.*
42. *Ibid.*, p. 47.
43. *Ibid.*, p. 142.

CHAPTER FOUR

1. See Albert Joseph George, *The Development of French Romanticism* (Syracuse: Syracuse University Press, 1955), p. 190 f.
2. Basil Willey, *The Seventeenth Century Background* (Garden City: Doubleday, 1955), p. 208.
3. Paul Hazard, *La Crise de la conscience européenne* (Paris: Boivin, 1935), p. 355.
4. Charles Baudelaire, *Les Fleurs du mal*, eds. Jacques Crépet and Georges Blin (Paris: Corti, 1950), p. 5.
5. *Ibid.*, p. 8.
6. *Ibid.*, p. 9.
7. Alfred de Vigny, "Dernière nuit de travail," in *Théâtre complet* (Paris: Jacottet, 1858), p. 4.
8. *Ibid.*, *Chatterton*, p. 31.
9. *Ibid.*, "Dernière nuit de travail," p. 5.

10. Vigny, *Poëmes*, in *Oeuvres complètes* (Paris: Conard, 1914), I, p. 8.
11. *Ibid.*, p. 239.
12. Pierre-Georges Castex, *Vigny: l'homme et l'oeuvre* (Paris: Boivin, 1952), p. 164.
13. Alfred de Vigny, *Journal d'un poète*, ed. Fernand Baldensperger (London: Scholartis, 1928), pp. 154-55.
14. *Ibid.*, p. 3.
15. *Ibid.*, p. 12.
16. *Ibid.*, p. 178.
17. Vigny, *Chatterton*, *op. cit.*, p. 30.
18. *Ibid.*, p. 83.
19. Alfred de Vigny, *Stello* (Paris: Lemerre, n.d.), p. 25.
20. Pierre Moreau, *Le Romantisme* (Paris: Gigord, 1932), p. 287.
21. Cf. Castex, p. 137.
22. Victor Hugo, *William Shakespeare*, in *Philosophie II, Oeuvres complètes* (Paris: Ollendorff, 1880), p. 42.
23. *Ibid.*, p. 314.
24. *Ibid.*, p. 159.
25. Paul Zumthor, *Victor Hugo: Poète de Satan* (Paris: Laffont, 1946), p. 160.
26. Emile Faguet, *Dix-neuvième siècle* (Paris: Société française d'imprimerie et de librairie, n.d.), pp. 191-92.
27. Victor Hugo, "Préface aux *Odes et ballades*," 1824, *Oeuvres complètes*, I, p. v.
28. Auguste Viatte, *Victor Hugo et les illuminés de son temps* (Ottawa: Editions de l'Arbre, 1942), pp. 245-56, elaborates this concept in detail.
29. Hugo, *William Shakespeare, op. cit.*, p. 141.
30. Zumthor, pp. 73-74.
31. *Ibid.*, pp. 63-64.
32. Hugo, *William Shakespeare*, p. 343.
33. *Ibid.*, p. 211.

34. *Ibid.*

35. Zumthor, p. 121.

36. Vigny, *Journal d'un poète*, p. 59.

37. Ernest Seillière, *Romantisme et démocratie romantique* (Paris: Nouvelle revue critique, 1930), pp. 113-14. Also cf. Faguet, p. 180.

38. See Viatte, p. 159 f.

39. Hugo, "Préface aux *Odes et ballades*," 1824, *op. cit.*, I, pp. 20-21.

40. Cf. Marcel Raymond, "Bergson et la poésie récente," in *Génies de France* (Neuchâtel: Editions de la Baconnière, 1942), p. 220. Consider the following remark on Bergson as indicative of the pre-symbolist mind which Hugo and Nerval represent: "Ces remarques préliminaires nous conduisent à un fait essentiel: l'anti-intellectualiste Bergson a désespéré du langage. Son optimisme quant aux pouvoirs de l'intuition s'accompagne d'un refus net de tout réalisme, de tout mysticisme linguistique. L'intuition, qui est vision directe de l'esprit par l'esprit, arrache les masques, rompt le réseau des habitudes; suffisamment purifiée, elle est capable d'atteindre le réel, l'absolu." See Viatte, *Troisième partie*, for a comprehensive discussion of Hugo's mysticism.

41. Gérard de Nerval, *Aurélia*, in *Oeuvres* (Paris: Gallimard, 1952), I, p. 359.

42. *Ibid.*, p. 267.

43. *Ibid.*, *Octavie*, 1, pp. 307-08.

44. See commentary, *ibid.*, "La Capharnaum," I, p. 124.

45. Ibid., *Aurélia*, I, p. 363.

46. Guy Michaud, *Message poétique du symbolisme* (Paris: Nizet, 1947), I, pp. 33-34.

47. See Francisque Vial and Louis Denise, *Idées et doctrines littéraires du XIX siècle* (Paris: Delagrave, 1928), p. 23.

48. Gérard de Nerval, *Les Chimères*, ed. Jeanine Moulin (Genève: Droz, 1949), p. xxvii.

49. Philippe van Tieghem, *Le Romantisme français* (Paris: Presses universitaires, 1947), p. 112.

CHAPTER FIVE

1. François-Auguste de Chateaubriand, *René* (Paris: Droz, 1935), pp. xv-xvi.

2. Victor Hugo, *Hernani*, in *Drame IV, Oeuvres complètes* (Paris: Ollendorff, 1926), p. 76.

3. *Ibid.*, p. 47.

4. Henri-Marie Beyle, *Le Rouge et le noir* (Paris: Crès, 1922), p. 361.

5. Alexandre Dumas *père*, *Antony*, in *Théâtre romantique* (Paris: Firmin-Didot, n.d.), p. 126.

6. Honoré de Balzac, *Le Père Goriot*, in *Oeuvres complètes* (Paris: Conard, 1912), p. 329.

7. *Ibid.*, p. 332.

8. *Ibid.*, pp. 515-16.

9. Edmond Estève, *Byron et le romantisme français* (Paris: Boivin, n.d.), p. 32.

10. *Ibid.*, pp. 37-38.

11. Paul Zumthor, *Victor Hugo: Poète de Satan* (Paris: Laffont, 1946), p. 131.

12. *Ibid.*, p. 258.

13. Alfred de Vigny, *Poëmes*, in *Oeuvres complètes* (Paris: Conard, 1914), I, p. 39.

14. Charles Baudelaire, *Les Fleurs du mal*, eds. Jacques Crépet and Georges Blin (Paris: Corti, 1950), p. 150.

15. *Ibid.*, p. 148.

16. *Ibid.*, p. 152.

17. Victor Hugo, *Han d'Islande*, in *Oeuvres complètes* (Paris: Ollendorff, 1926), p. 514.

18. *Ibid.*, p. 521.

19. *Ibid.*, p. 522.

20. N. H. Clement, *Romanticism in France* (New York: MLA, 1939), pp. 428-29.

21. Jules Barbey d'Aurevilly, *Du Dandysme et de Georges Brummell* (Paris: Emile-Paul, 1918), pp. 12-15.
22. *Ibid.*, pp. 16-17.
23. Baudelaire, p. 20.
24. Jean Canu, *Barbey d'Aurevilly* (Paris: Laffont, 1945), p. 90.
25. Clement, p. 476.
26. Jules Barbey d'Aurevilly, *Les Diaboliques* (Paris: Lemerre, 1934), p. 90.
27. *Ibid.*, p. 216.
28. *Ibid.*, p. 342.
29. Canu, pp. 91-92.
30. Charles Baudelaire, *L'Art romantique* (Paris: Conard, 1925), p. 89.
31. *Ibid.*, pp. 90-91.

CHAPTER SIX

1. Alfred de Musset, *Premières poésies* (Paris: Garnier, n.d.), p. 199.
2. Théophile Gautier, "Albertus," in *Poésies complètes* (Paris: Charpentier, 1922), p. 172.
3. *Ibid.*, p. 184.
4. Pétrus Borel, *Contes immoraux* (Amsterdam: Société des bibliophiles, 1870), p. 43.

5. Prosper Mérimée, *Chronique du règne de Charles IX* (Paris: Charpentier, 1847), pp. 272-73.
6. Alfred de Musset, *Comédies et proverbes* (Paris: Garnier, 1923), pp. 405-06.
7. *Ibid.*, p. 430.
8. *Ibid.*, p. 367.
9. *Ibid.*, p. 371.
10. *Ibid.*, p. 232.
11. *Ibid.*, p. 276.
12. *Ibid.*
13. *Ibid.*, p. 15.
14. *Ibid.*, p. 24.
15. *Ibid.*, p. 43.
16. *Ibid.*, p. 310.
17. *Ibid.*, pp. 285-86.
18. *Ibid.*, p. 283.
19. *Ibid.*, p. 290.
20. *Ibid.*, p. 292.
21. *Ibid.*, p. 306.
22. *Ibid.*, p. 320.
23. *Ibid.*, p. 323.
24. *Ibid.*, p. 328.
25. Victor Hugo, *Ruy Blas,* in *Oeuvres complètes* (Paris: Ollendorff, 1926), p. 105.
26. *Ibid.*, p. 177.
27. *Ibid.*, pp. 184-85.

INDEX

THIS is primarily an index of romantic heroes, not an author-title-subject index. Poems are listed under the poet's name, and title entries are made only when the protagonists of these works are not cardinal examples of the hero.

Adolphe, 36-37, 56-57, 62-63, 64-67, 115, 132
"Albertus," 116-17
André del Sarto, 121-22
Anthony, 38-39, 100, 114
d'Aurevilly, Barbey, 52, 60, 61, 109-10, 111-13, 134
Baudelaire, Charles, 94
    "L'Albatros," 78
    "Bénédiction," 34, 78
    "Bohémiens en voyage," 29
    "A Celle qui est trop gaie," 70
    "Les Correspondances," 69-70
    "Don Juan aux enfers," 110
    "Elévation," 79
    "L'Ennemi," 71
    "L'Héautontimorouménos," 70
    "L'Invitation au voyage," 29
    "Les Litanies de Satan," 106
    "Le Mauvais moine," 72
    "Le Peintre de la vie moderne," 113
    "Le Reniement de Saint Pierre," 105

    "Réversibilité," 72
    "Le Voyage," 28-29, 30
    "Voyage à Cythère," 72
Bug-Jargal, 43-44, 132
Les Caprices de Marianne, 120
Cécile, 37-38
Chatterton, 34-35, 48, 79-80
Chronique du règne de Charles IX, 117, 134
La Confession d'un enfant du siècle, 67, 71
Contes immoraux, 117
"La Coupe et les lèvres," 116
Fantasio, 122-26, 135
Han d'Islande, 106-08, 114
Hernani, 8-9, 42-43, 98-99, 114, 134
Hugo, Victor, 83-89, 92, 94
    Dieu, 85, 103
    La Fin de Satan, 85, 103
    "La Fonction du poète," 86
    La Légende des siècles, 85, 103
    "Les Mages," 86

Lamartine, Alphonse de
  La Chute d'un ange, 103
  Satan Sauvé, 103
Lambert, Louis, 10-11
Nerval, Gérard de, 64-65, 74, 89-94, 131-32
  Aurélia, 35, 90, 92-93, 94
  "Delfica," 26
  "Myrtho," 26
  Octavie, 27, 91
La Nuit vénitienne, 118
Obermann, 19-22, 57, 63, 68, 131
On ne badine pas avec l'amour, 119
Peau de chagrin, 50-51
Rastignac, Eugène de, 51, 100-02, 104, 134

René, 7-8, 16-19, 39-42, 55-56, 97-98, 131
Ruy Blas, 115, 126-28
Servitude et grandeur militaires, 23
Sorel, Julien, 57-59, 63-64, 99-100, 114, 132, 134
Stello, 35, 80-81
Valentin, Raphaël, 50-51
Vigny, Alfred de, 68-69, 80, 92, 94, 133
  "La Bouteille à la mer," 24, 81-82
  "Les Destinées," 45-46
  "La Maison du berger," 24
  "Moïse," 24, 81
Eloa, 46-47, 104
Le Journal d'un poète, 81